**Prentice-Hall Series in Foodservice Management**

Coltman, *Food and Beverage Cost Control*

Danenburg, Moncrief, and Taylor,
    *Introduction to Wholesale Distribution*

Kahrl, *Introduction to Modern Food and Beverage Service*

Kahrl, *Advanced Modern Food and Beverage Service*

Keister, *Food and Beverage Control*

Levinson, *Food and Beverage Operation:
    Cost Control and Systems Management*

# Food and Beverage Cost Control

## Michael M. Coltman

*British Columbia
Institute of Technology*

Prentice-Hall, Inc., Englewood Cliffs, New Jersey 07632

*Library of Congress Cataloging in Publication Data*

Coltman, Michael M  (date)
    Food and beverage cost control.

    Includes index.
    1. Food service—Cost control.  I. Title.
TX911.3.C65C64        658.1'552        76-16783
ISBN 0-13-323006-6

Printed in the United States of America

10  9  8  7  6  5  4  3

Prentice-Hall International, Inc., London
Prentice-Hall of Australia Pty. Ltd., Sydney
Prentice-Hall of Canada, Ltd., Toronto
Prentice-Hall of India Private Limited, New Delhi
Prentice-Hall of Japan, Inc., Tokyo
Prentice-Hall of Southeast Asia Pty. Ltd., Singapore
Whitehall Books Limited, Wellington, New Zealand

*This book is dedicated to my wife, Theresa*

# Contents

# 3

# Food Purchasing                                              41

# 4

# Receiving and the Receiving Report                          53

# 5

# Food Stores and Inventory Control                           67

# 6

# Receiving Report Summary                   *87*

# 7

# Food Production                             *107*

# 8

# Evaluation of Food Cost Results            *135*

# 9
# Beverage Cost Control: The Storeroom                                            165

# 10
# Beverage Cost Control: The Bar                                                  183

# Glossary                                                                        211

# Index                                                                          219

# Preface

The food and beverage industry includes not only food and beverage departments in hotels, but also independent restaurants, chain food operations, department store restaurants, industrial and hospital catering, and many related types of businesses. It is a large and growing industry, and one that is as prone to the cost squeeze as any other. One method of combating this squeeze is to increase selling prices as cost prices increase. Alternatively, more attention could be paid to costs in order to control them more carefully so that unnecessary increases in selling prices are not required. This book, therefore, is primarily concerned with descriptions, illustrations, and explanations of systems that can be implemented to control two of the major costs of the industry: food and alcoholic beverages.

The book is not exhaustive. It does not include every possible control technique or method (some organizations, indeed, have control systems unique to their own particular company). It does, however, include those systems which have been found to be in most common use. Variations of some of the systems described will, no doubt, be found in some establishments. Furthermore, the book does not suggest that all the systems described should, or could, be used in every food and/or beverage operation. In smaller establishments, for example, many systems could be simplified to keep the cost of control to a minimum. The reader must therefore use discretion in implementing the controls best suited to each size and type of organization.

The control of food and beverages can be visualized as a control of the *processing* of these items. In other words, what happens to the goods at each stage of processing—purchasing, receiving, storing, production, and selling? What can be done at each stage to minimize losses and have information that tells us whether or not the costs we end up with are the ones we should have? It was with these questions in mind that the book was written.

Chapter 1 is an introduction. Chapter 2 deals with control of sales (revenue). The control of food is covered in chapters 3 to 8. The control of alcoholic beverages is discussed in the final two chapters, 9 and 10.

The book has been written for the general reader who is in, or is planning to enter, the food and/or beverage business. Students who are preparing for a career in this industry should also find the book practical. For this latter group, questions and problems have been included at the end of each chapter.

I would like to sincerely thank a teaching colleague, Bob Brett, who willingly gave invaluable time in reading drafts of this text and offered innumerable useful suggestions for improving the material.

# 1
# Introduction

One of the commonly used measures for assessing success in business is return on investment. Many businesses, and in particular many restaurants, fail because sales are not high enough to cover all costs and create a profit. But many restaurant failures are explained by an unsatisfactory level of sales when, in fact, the reason is not that sales were too low, but that *costs were too high* for the volume of sales achieved. Therefore, the major emphasis in this book will be on controlling the cost of food and beverages.

The word "control" is not intended to imply manipulation or suppression of people; rather, it has the connotation of a management information system. Management's job is to make decisions, and rational decisions can only be made with appropriate information. Management needs information about costs of food and beverages, inventory levels, quality of purchases and of food produced, sales prices and sales levels — to list just a few. Only with an information system, with control, can proper decisions be made.

## AMOUNT OF CONTROL

The *amount* of control is related to the size of the establishment. A small restaurant cannot afford, nor does it need, the same amount of control and information as a multidepartment food and beverage complex in a 1,000-room hotel. But even a large hotel must put some limits on the volume of data that can be provided with today's computerized accounting systems. A couple of aspirins can help cure a headache; a hundred might well kill the patient.

## KINDS OF INFORMATION

Information must therefore be *selective*. It is of little value for management to know, each day, exactly the quantity on hand of every individual item in the food storeroom; but a monthly calculation of total value of food inventory can provide a very useful decision-making tool — inventory turnover, which will be discussed in Chapter 5.

Information provided by the control system must be acted upon *if* action is called for. It is useless to have the accounting department produce a daily food cost percentage calculation that shows a steadily rising cost if management only takes action after the monthly income and expenditure statement is prepared.

Information that would be valuable to those who are in a position to take action to correct or improve a situation should be promptly communicated to those people. If management is provided with a daily food cost figure by the accounting office, then this figure should also be made available to the chef, since he is the one usually responsible for meeting the food cost goal.

## SYSTEM GOALS

What are some of the goals that can be achieved by a good control/information system?

1. *Performance and quality can be standardized.* By having written procedures for such things as recipes for food and beverage production, performance can be standardized and quality controlled.

2. *Assets can be safeguarded.* Proper forms, records, and controls can safeguard assets (such as cash or inventory) from theft, wastage or misuse.

3. *Performance can be measured.* Key indicators, such as food cost percentage, beverage cost percentage, and inventory turnover rate, can be invaluable measuring devices.

4. *Planning can be made easier.* Historical records of costs of food and beverages, and records of customer preferences, help in planning for the future.

## Limitations

An understanding of the limitations of controls is necessary. Controls:

Do *not* substitute for management supervision. A control system, even a good one, still requires supervision to ensure that it is functioning correctly.

Do *not* cure problems. They only point out that problems do or do not exist; then it is management's task to take any necessary action.

Are *not* an end in themselves, but only a means to an end. Having a watertight control system to achieve the lowest food cost in town is not very profitable if the dining room is empty most meal periods.

Are *not*, to repeat, devices for policing employees. They should be considered akin to a health campaign, the purpose of which is not to cure the unwell but rather to prevent sickness.

## THE FOOD AND BEVERAGE CONTROL DEPARTMENT

In a large hotel or food operation with its own accounting department, the food and beverage control personnel form a branch of that department. Even though this branch is responsible to the accountant for details related to accounting and control procedures, it must work with the personnel of the food and beverage department, such as the food and beverage manager, the executive chef, and other departmental managers. It is important that this cooperation be reciprocated if an effective job is to be done.

Because the food and beverage manager is ultimately responsible for food and beverage costs, the records, reports, and recommendations prepared by the control office must be made available to the key operating people of the food and beverage department. Control office personnel must not, however, interfere with the day-to-day operations of the food and beverage department. The control office should also prepare whatever analyses and special reports the food and beverage manager requires.

It is obvious that food and beverage control is more than just a desk job; anyone involved in it must have not only a basic knowledge of accounting, but also experience in purchasing, preparation, and even service. In relatively small operations, where only an owner-manager and/or chef may be involved, the same objectives and principles apply; it is just the procedures that will be simplified.

### Main Duties and Responsibilities

The following might be the main duties and responsibilities of the food and beverage control department:

1. *Sales.* To establish revenue (sales) control procedures to ensure that all food and beverages are properly priced and recorded as sold, and to ensure that all revenue is accounted for; to analyze sales by department, meal period, and menu item.

2. *Purchasing.* To assist in establishing purchase specifications and procedures for food and beverages and to ensure, by periodic review, that these specifications are being adhered to and that procedures are being followed.

3. *Receiving.* To establish receiving procedures and ensure that they are continually followed.

4. *Storing and Issuing.* To establish storeroom control procedures and a system for issuing items from stores into production.

5. *Inventory.* To supervise the taking and calculation of all food and beverage inventories on a monthly (or more frequent) basis.

6. *Production.* To work with the chef in food tests to attain an acceptable yield on menu items, and to prepare standard recipe cost information; to work with the bar manager to achieve the same objectives for bar drinks and cocktails; to establish portion controls and see that they are adhered to.

7. *Reports.* To prepare daily, weekly, and monthly information reports related to any or all of the above six items that management requires for information and subsequent decision-making purposes.

## EXTERNAL INFORMATION

So far only *internal* controls and information have been mentioned. For the most part, this book will be limited to such matters, but there are two areas of *external* information that must not be ignored by management: (1) *competitive information* — what is the competition doing, and what is happening in the marketplace? and (2) *environmental information* — what is the current and future status of the social, political, and economic "climate" in which the hotel or restaurant operates? In these changing times, a manager cannot operate successfully by looking only at the internal situation.

## SUMMARY

To succeed in business, an adequate return on investment is required; to achieve it, a satisfactory level of sales must be maintained and costs must be controlled. Costs can be controlled by having a good information system. Only with proper information about costs can management make the right decisions. The amount of control required depends on the size and type of operation, but the information provided by any control system should be limited to what is practical and useful, should be acted upon when action is called for, and should be communicated to all those involved.

With good controls, performance and quality can be standardized, assets can be safeguarded, performance can be measured, and planning can be made easier. But controls do have limitations. They are not substitutes for management supervision or cures for problems; nor are they an end in themselves or an employee policing device.

Despite the fact that those involved in food and beverage control are employees of the accounting department, they must work harmoniously with other employees and department heads in food and beverage production and service. The main duties and responsibilities of those involved in food and beverage control are to institute routines and procedures for the following major areas: sales, purchasing, receiving, storing and issuing, inventory, and production.

Finally, even though cost control is primarily an internal problem, one should always be cognizant of external factors that could have an effect on costs.

## DISCUSSION QUESTIONS

1. Why is controlling costs sometimes more important than increasing sales?

2. Why does management need an information system?

3. Why should management communicate information to key personnel at the department level?

4. What are some of the goals that can be met with a good control/information system?

5. What are some of the limitations of a control system?

6. What *external* factors must a manager keep in mind in order to make good business decisions?

① bee. maximum level of sales can't be realized w/o being able to control costs. ∴ realizing maximum profit.

① To enable them to make right decision w/ regards cost control

③ to take action to correct or improve a situation shld. be communicated to the employees.

④ - performance & quality can be standardized
   - assets safeguarded
   - performance can be measured
   - planning can be made easier.

⑤ - not a subst. type to management supervision
   - not an end in itself, rather a means to an end.
   - not a device for policing employee
   - do not cure problems.

# 2

# Sales (Revenue) Control

## Objectives

After studying this chapter, the reader will be able to

1. Identify the two main reasons why sales checks are important to food sales control.

2. List the names of the four basic forms required for a system of manual food and beverage sales control, and give a one-sentence explanation of each form.

3. Carry out a step-by-step daily audit of sales control with a manual system; list errors discovered and possible causes; and suggest solutions to eliminate such errors in the future.

4. List the advantages of machine systems over manual systems and describe the principal features of the following machines: precheck, preset precheck, electronic.

5. Calculate the amount of an average check (average cover) and identify whether a trend in the amount is desirable or not.

6. Separate the tax amount where such tax is included in the food or beverage total.

7. List the four basic records (forms) required for banquet sales control and give a one-sentence description of the purpose of each.

Basic to any sales control system, either for food or for beverages, is the use of sales checks on which the server records the items sold and their prices. Without sales checks, even if all the revenue that an establishment is supposed to get is properly received, there would be no record of *what has been sold* and in *what quantities.* As will be seen later, this information is important for controlling costs.

There are circumstances in which it would be impractical to record items sold on a sales check for each customer or group of customers. An example – and there are others – would be a cafeteria, where the customer serves him or herself and pays a cashier at the end of the line. Control over revenue in this situation is achieved by the customer paying only what he sees rung up in the cash register (although this does not necessarily eliminate all possibilities of loss). If it is necessary for production purposes to know the quantity of major menu items sold, this can be done by having operating keys on the register coded to individual menu items. These operating keys are connected to counters that register one more digit each time the key is depressed.

Alternatively, a record of quantity sold can be made manually by the cashier by the use of a *scatter sheet.* A scatter sheet, illustrated in Figure 2.1, is simply a listing of the menu

| October 1 | | | |
|---|---|---|---|
| Hamburger | ⁄⁄⁄⁄ ⁄⁄⁄⁄ ⁄⁄⁄⁄ | // | 42 |
| Flank Steak | ⁄⁄⁄⁄ ⁄⁄⁄⁄ ⁄⁄⁄⁄ ⁄⁄ | | 24 |
| Sole | ⁄⁄⁄⁄ /// | | 8 |
| Chicken Legs | ⁄⁄⁄⁄ ⁄⁄⁄⁄ ⁄⁄⁄⁄ ⁄⁄⁄⁄ | ⁄⁄⁄⁄ /// | 53 |
| Veal Stew | ⁄⁄⁄⁄ ⁄⁄⁄⁄ ⁄⁄⁄⁄ //// | | 19 |

**Figure 2.1** Scatter sheet.

items for the day or meal period, which is filled in by the cashier as each customer pays for the food items. Such records of day-by-day sales of various menu items are of great help to the chef in planning production quantities when the same items are to be offered on the menu on some future day. In most cases, how-ever, quantities sold should be recorded on sales checks.

There are two basic approaches to recording and con-trolling food and beverage sales – a manual system and a machine system. These will be discussed in turn.

## MANUAL SYSTEMS

The following are required in a *manual system* for recording sales of food or beverages:

1. Sequentially prenumbered sales checks
2. Duplicates of sales checks for ordering food from the kitchen or beverages from the bar
3. A record of which servers have received which blank books of sales checks and duplicates
4. Columnar journal sheets for summarizing sales

### Sales Checks

Sales checks are available in a multitude of styles and varieties, but the basic arrangement is to provide space for writing quantities of items ordered, descriptions of items, prices, exten-sions, and total dollar amount. There may also be space for record-ing the server's identifying number or letter and the number of

**Figure 2.2** In addition to control of the cost of food and beverages, control of their sale is also important. Photograph courtesy Hyatt Regency Hotel, Vancouver, B.C.

guests served. Sales checks should be sequentially prenumbered. Figure 2.3 shows a basic sales check for a dining room that serves alcoholic beverages.

*Duplicates*

In dining room situations, duplicates are required for ordering food from the kitchen and/or drinks from the bar. These duplicates serve a number of purposes:

1. They provide the kitchen or bar with a written record of what is required.
2. They authorize the kitchen or bar to issue the food or drink to the server.
3. If the original of the sales check is subsequently lost or destroyed, the duplicates will help to determine the amount of the sale.

These duplicates may or may not have the same preprinted number as the original sales check. If they have different numbers, then they should be cross-referenced to the original by the waiter or waitress handwriting the original sales check number on the duplicate, and vice versa.

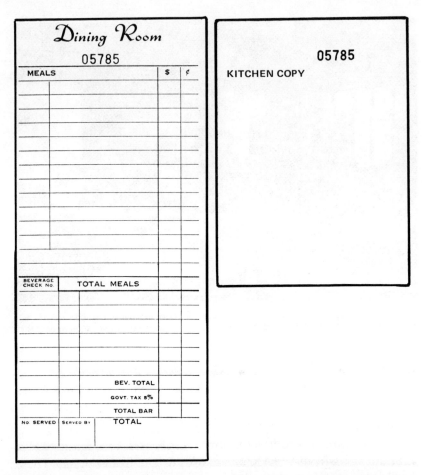

**Figure 2.3** Sample of blank Sales Check and kitchen duplicate (order copy). Separate duplicates would be required for ordering beverages from the bar. They may have a different number sequence, in which case the numbers will have to be cross referenced.

In some situations, for example in a bar, duplicates may be dispensed with (this saves on cost and paperwork) by having the server give the original to the bartender so that he can prepare the drinks; the server then gets back this sales check when he or she picks up the drinks for presentation to the customer. Some control may be lost with this procedure.

*Record of Checks Issued*

All prenumbered checks and duplicates should be controlled. Blank pads of checks can be issued to servers by the dining room or bar manager or by a cashier. A control book or form is necessary in order to know who is responsible for missing sales checks. This control form is illustrated in Figure 2.4.

## Sales Summary Record

One of the ways of summarizing sales in a manual system is to have used sales checks listed on a columnar journal sheet by the cashier. A sample sales check journal sheet is illustrated in Figure 2.5. At the end of the shift or the day, the cash on hand should balance with the Cash Total column. In a hotel, cashiers should send all charge checks to the front office so that guests can have the amount added to their bills, and "city ledger" accounts can be made up for other credit card customers. If no charges are permitted in the restaurant, then that part of the sheet can be eliminated.

In some dining room and/or bar situations, there is no cashier. Each waiter or waitress is responsible for collecting cash from customers and for keeping this cash and all sales checks until the end of the shift. Under these circumstances the use of journal sheets could be bypassed by simply making an adding machine available. Each waiter or waitress can add up all sales checks at the end of the shift and turn in sales checks, adding machine tape, and cash.

| CHECK NUMBER ISSUE CONTROL FORM | | | | |
|---|---|---|---|---|
| DATE | Checks Issued | Waiter/Waitress Signature | Last Number Used | Cashier Signature |
| Oct. 1 | 1026 – 1050 | D. Dovier | 1043 | W. Jores |
| | 947 – 950 | L. Scofield | 950 | W. Jores |
| | 951 – 1000 | L. Scofield | 974 | W. Jones |
| | 1212 – 1250 | R. Evans | 1231 | W. Jores |
| | 1463 – 1500 | J. Hartley | 1482 | W. Jones |
| | 1117 – 1150 | W. Stansdose | 1140 | W. Jores |
| Oct. 2 | 1044 – 1050 | B Dovier | 1050 | Daniels |
| | 1051 – 1100 | B. Dovier | 1062 | Daniels |
| | 975 – 1000 | L. Scofield | 996 | Daniels |
| | 1232 – 1250 | R. Evans | 1249 | Daniels |

**Figure 2.4** When blank books of sales checks are issued to servers, they sign for their receipt. Unused checks turned in at the end of the period are signed for by the cashier.

| SALES CHECK JOURNAL SHEET | | DATE *Oct. 1* SHIFT *A.M.* CASHIER *W Jones* | | | | | | | | |
|---|---|---|---|---|---|---|---|---|---|---|
| Check # | Waiter # | CASH | | | | CHARGE | | | | | |
| | | Food | Bev. | Other | TOTAL | Food | Bev. | Gratuity | Other | TOTAL | Charge Information |
| 1026 | 4 | 4.00 | 2.00 | | 6.00 | | | | | | |
| 952 | 3 | | | | | 14.20 | 3.10 | 2.00 | | 19.30 | Room 1437 |
| 1028 | 2 | 1.00 | | | 1.00 | | | | | | |
| 1213 | 5 | 9.40 | 0.75 | | 10.15 | | | | | | |
| 1463 | 7 | | | | | 3.25 | | 0.50 | | 3.75 | Room 929 |
| 1095 | | | | | | | | | | | |
| | | | | | | | | | | | |
| | | | | | | | | | | | |
| | | | | | | | | | | | |
| T O T A L S | | 217.95 | 51.10 | | 269.05 | 91.10 | 17.70 | 15.50 | | 124.30 | |

**Figure 2.5** Journal sheet for summarizing sales at the end of meal period or day. Cash sales information should be kept separate from charge information. Cashier's remittance should be balanced to Cash Total column.

Another way of avoiding the use of journal sheets where there is a cashier on duty is to provide a cash register that validates each check as it is presented for payment and accumulates separate totals for food, beverage, tax, and total sales. To overcome the possibility of sales checks being overrung, underrung, or rung wrongly, it is usually necessary for the control office each day to take separate adding machine totals directly from the sales checks turned in and verify these totals against the register readings. Total cash turned in should also be in agreement with the adding machine total of all cash sales checks.

### Control Office Responsibilities

The following routine should be carried out on a daily basis:

1. Spot-check prices, extensions, and additions of sales checks. (Cashiers could be instructed to verify these items as the check is presented for payment.)

2. Ensure that each check is properly listed on the sales check journal sheet, or on the adding machine tape if each server acts as his/her own cashier.

3. Add up sales check journal sheet columns and cross-foot the column totals to ensure, for example, that Food + Beverage + Other = Total.

4. Reconcile cash remittances with the sales check journal sheet Cash Total column, or with adding machine tape total.

5. Ensure that there are no missing sales checks by sorting them into number sequence (if servers act also as cashiers, they can be instructed to do this before adding up sales checks). Watch particularly for missing numbers between the last one in each series used on the preceding day and the first one used on the current day. A useful form for controlling numbers is illustrated in Figure 2.6.

## Missing Sales Checks

If servers are made responsible for ensuring that no sales checks leave the premises inadvertently with customers, there is still the problem of determining if the cashier or the server is at fault for a "missing" check. One way to pinpoint responsibility is to have a perforated stub attached either to the top or bottom of the original. This stub will have the same preprinted number on it as the original. As the check is presented to the cashier by the server, along with the cash collected from the guest, the cashier has only to validate the stub with a rubber stamp, date stamp, or other printing device. If a check is subsequently missing

| SALES CHECK LIST | | | | | |
|---|---|---|---|---|---|
| 101 | 151 | 201 | 251 | 301 | 351 |
| 102 | 152 | 202 | 252 | 302 | 352 |
| 103 | 153 | 203 | 253 | 303 | 353 |
| 104 | 154 | 204 | 254 | 304 | 354 |
| 105 | 155 | 205 | 255 | 305 | 355 |
| 106 | 156 | 206 | 256 | 306 | 356 |
| 107 | 157 | 207) ? | 257 | 307 | 357 |
| 108 | 158 | 208 | 258 | 308 | 358 |
| 109 | 159 | 209 | 259 | 309 | 359 |
| 110 | 160 | 210 | 260 | 310 | 360 |
| 111 | 161 | 211 | 261 | 311 | 361 |
| 112 | 162 | 212 | 262 | 312 | 362 |
| 113 | 163 | 213 | 263 | 313 | 363 |
| | | | 264 | 314 | 364 |

**Figure 2.6**  As used sales checks are turned in, they can be crossed off daily against this list, and any missing checks will be quickly spotted.

and the server has the receipted stub, then he or she is obviously not at fault and the cashier must be held accountable.

The amount of loss from a missing check can be determined by referring to the related duplicates in the kitchen and/or bar. These duplicates should be turned in daily, along with the originals, to the control office. The duplicates are generally used only on a spot-check basis (to verify that something ordered on a duplicate has not been left off the original), or to calculate the amount of loss from missing originals.

If a sales check is lost *after* it is turned in to the cashier and the check is designed with a server receipt stub (see preceding section), the amount of loss can be determined by referring to this stub. The stubs would have to be designed so that the total dollar amount of the sales check can be recorded on them.


## MACHINE SYSTEMS

Machine systems are generally of the *pre check* type. Precheck machines eliminate many of the problems and much of the work required in manual systems. For example, with a precheck machine sales checks do not need to be prenumbered, and a check number control form (Figure 2.4) is not required. Duplicates of sales checks are not needed, nor are sales check journal sheets (Figure 2.5). Finally, a cashier is not essential because each server can act as his or her own cashier.

### The Precheck Machine

Precheck machines or registers are generally designed to operate only when a sales check is inserted in the machine. Each server has his or her own machine operating key. To operate the machine with a check inserted, the server depresses descriptive keys, dollar amount keys, and finally his or her individual machine operating key. This last operation causes the machine to issue a duplicate that the waiter or waitress can then use to obtain food from the kitchen or beverages from the bar. For each transaction, the machine also prints a sequential number on both the original sales check and the duplicate, so the two are cross-referenced if questions arise later. All transactions are also recorded on a continuous "audit" tape that can only be removed from the machine at each day's end, by the control office, at the time the machine is "cleared."

The advantage of such a precheck system (and thus the use of the prefix *pre*) is that the sales check is made out, and the machine has recorded in it, the amount of the sale *before* the items are ordered from the kitchen or bar. At the end of each shift or day, machine readings can be taken to determine dollar sales by type of item and total dollar sales by each server.

A cashier is not required because each waiter or waitress can act as his or her own cashier, keeping cash collected from customers until the end of the shift. At that time the machine, when the appropriate keys are operated, will give a reading of each server's total dollar sales. That amount, adjusted for any corrections and reduced by the value of any charge sales checks handled by that server, will be the amount of cash that must be turned in.

There are machines that will print food items in one column of the sales check and liquor items in a separate column; that can add up each column separately, or simply give a combined total for food and beverages; that can be designed with a pickup balance feature to avoid addition errors by servers. Minor disadvantages are that the server can still make mistakes in pricing items, and/or that double writing may be required on the duplicate to give the kitchen or bar more detailed information.

### The Preset Precheck

An improvement over the basic precheck machine is the preset precheck machine. The keyboard of this machine has an additional number of keys (up to thirty-six) that make possible automatic pricing on the sales check and additional descriptive wording about the menu item that reduces the amount of handwriting by servers. The price is preprogramed into the machine for each separate menu item, thus eliminating pricing errors by servers. A remote-control panel, kept under lock and key, allows management to change the price of any one of the thirty-six menu items in seconds, thus giving pricing flexibility. An optional feature of the machine is that thirty-six "activity" counters (one for each of the menu items) will keep a running count of each item recorded upon depression of its corresponding preset key, thus giving at a glance a total, by meal period or by

**Figure 2.7** The precheck machine for recording sales is designed to operate only if a sales check is inserted in the printing table on the left side. Photograph courtesy The National Cash Register Company, Dayton, Ohio.

day, of the quantities of each menu item sold. These preset precheck machines can be used in a food operation, a bar operation, or in a combined food-bar sales outlet.

### Electronic Registers

High-speed electronic sales registers were developed primarily for high-volume, limited-menu restaurants and fast food operations requiring detailed sales analyses. These registers can also be used in dining rooms, bars, and cocktail lounges. As well as having up to 120 preset price keys, the registers offer such features as these:

1. Price "lookup" for up to sixty prices. With automatic price lookup, there is no need for a server to refer to lists or menus for prices of special promotion items, since the register has this information stored in its memory.

2. Automatic tax calculation, which eliminates manually calculating different tax rates for, for example, food eaten on the premises or food taken out.

**Figure 2.8** Electronic cash registers have been recently introduced. In addition to other innovative features, they offer many more preset prices and waiter/waitress totals. Photograph courtesy The National Cash Register Company, Dayton, Ohio.

3. Automatic price changes during special promotion periods. By entering a special code number at the time the sales check is being prepared, the server can instruct the machine to change the normal preset price to a special price (which the machine has stored in its memory). Such a feature might be desirable during the so-called happy hour in a cocktail lounge.

4. Additional descriptive keys that permit the register to provide such detailed information as how many steaks were ordered rare, medium, or well-done; or how many milkshakes of various flavors were served.

The register is also capable of storing inventory information under management control; an inventory count of selected menu items can be maintained and updated on a daily basis. Automatic change computation and coin dispensing can also be added.

## THE AVERAGE CHECK (OR COVER)

Regardless of the system, whether manual or machine, a useful sales statistic that can be calculated daily by sales outlet, and

| DAILY SALES REPORT | | ITEM COUNT | REGISTER TOTALS | |
|---|---|---|---|---|
| START #52  PROGRAM CHANGE/RESET COUNTER CUSTOMER COUNTER/NO SALE | X | 51 | 361 | C |
| | X | 621 | 22 | C |
| Hamburger | X | 112 | 39.78 | 1C |
| Deluxe Hamburger | X | 61 | 35.99 | 2C |
| Double Hamburger | X | 23 | 18.17 | 3C |
| Cheese Burger | X | 74 | 36.26 | 4C |
| Double Cheese Burger | X | 19 | 16.81 | 5C |
| Whopper | X | 12 | 11.88 | 6C |
| Super Burger | X | 8 | 7.92 | 7C |
| Beef | X | 31 | 27.59 | 8C |
| Chili Burger | X | 10 | 5.90 | 9C |
| Ribs | X | 18 | 35.82 | 10C |
| Chicken | X | 29 | 46.11 | 11C |
| White Chicken | X | 5 | 8.45 | 12C |
| Dark Chicken | X | 5 | 7.45 | 13C |
| Barrel | X | 3 | 14.67 | 14C |
| Bucket | | | | |
| | | 11 | 3.90 | 55C |
| Mashed Potatoes | X | 14 | 4.20 | 56C |
| Potato Salad | X | 21 | 6.30 | 57C |
| Salad | X | 32 | 16.00 | 58C |
| Bread | X | 36 | 3.60 | 59C |
| Rolls | X | 21 | 2.10 | 60C |
| Soup | X | 3 | .90 | 61C |
| Pie | X | 32 | 14.40 | 62C |
| French Fries | X | 123 | 36.90 | 63C |
| Iced Tea | X | 41 | 6.15 | 64C |
| Hot Chocolate | X | 6 | .90 | 65C |
| Coffee | X | 179 | 17.90 | 66C |
| Cola | X | 312 | 62.40 | 67C |
| Milk | X | 26 | 7.80 | 68C |
| Hot Tea | X | 4 | .60 | 69C |
| Orange | X | 41 | 6.15 | 70C |
| NET PRESET SALES | X | | 926.09 | 71C |
| MISCELLANEOUS | X | 3 | 11.85 | 72C |
| SPECIAL | X | 1 | 4.50 | 73C |
| TOTAL NET SALES | X | | 942.44 | 74C |
| GROSS SALES | X | | 971.15 | 75C |
| | X | | | |
| CONSECUTIVE # / STORE & REGISTER # / DATE | X | 2280 | 12 | 4/02/7- |

**Figure 2.9** Illustration of a management report available from electronic register — a sales breakdown for a fast food operation of up to seventy different menu items. Courtesy The National Cash Register Company, Dayton, Ohio.

even by meal period, is the *average check* or *average cover*. This is the amount of money spent on average by each guest. It can be identified for food only, for beverage only, or for combined food and beverage. (If any tax is included in the sales amount, this should be separated out before calculating the average because the tax has to be forwarded to a government agency and is not revenue to the establishment. The method for separating this tax amount is discussed in the next section.) The method for calculating the average check is as follows:

$$\text{Average check} = \frac{\text{Total sales}}{\text{Number of guests}}$$

| NET REGISTER TOTAL | |
|---|---|
| START #50 PROGRAM CHANGE/RESET COUNTER CUSTOMER COUNTER/NO SALE | X    51          361      A |
| NET ACCOUNTABILITY | X  621           22      A<br>X    1      925.25  A A |
| CONSECUTIVE #/STORE & REGISTER #/DATE | 2278      12  4/02/7- |

| REGISTER FINANCIAL REPORT | | TRANS COUNT | REGISTER TOTALS |
|---|---|---|---|
| START #51 PROGRAM CHANGE/RESET COUNTER CUSTOMER COUNTER/NO SALE | | X   51 | 361        B |
| | | X  621 | 22        B |
| CURRENT TIED—UP GROUP | 1B | X | 30637.45      1B |
| GROSS SALES TODAY | 2B | X | 971.15      2B |
| DEPARTMENT VOIDS | 3B | X    0 | .00      3B |
| DISCOUNTS | 4B | X    0 | .00      4B |
| NET SALES | 5B | X | 971.15      5B |
| PAID OUT | 6B | X    5 | 45.90      6B |
| CASH CALLED FOR | 7B | X | 925.25      7B |
| INSIDE SALES TOTAL | 8B | X  461 | 648.93      8B |
| CARRYOUT SALES TOTAL | 9B | X  160 | 322.22      9B |
| CONSECUTIVE #/STORE & REGISTER #/DATE | | 2279 | 12  4/02/7- |

| TAXABLE GROUP TOTAL REPORT | |
|---|---|
| START #53 PROGRAM CHANGE/RESET COUNTER CUSTOMER COUNTER/NO SALE | X   51          361      D |
| TAXABLE GROUP TOTAL                   1F | X  621           22      D<br>X           338.57    ID |
| CONSECUTIVE #/STORE & REGISTER #/DATE | 2281    12  4/02/7 |

**Figure 2.10** Management report printout information available with an electronic register. Courtesy The National Cash Register Company, Dayton, Ohio.

Total food sales according to our sales check journal sheet (Figure 2.5) on October 1 were

| | |
|---|---|
| Cash | $217.95 |
| Charge | $ 91.10 |
| Total | $309.05 |

Assuming the total number of guests served was 147, our average food check for this period on October 1 would be

$$\frac{\$309.05}{147} = \$2.10$$

In establishments where management wishes to have an average check calculated, the sales check should be designed so that the number of customers served can be recorded. The sales check journal sheet (if a manual system is in effect) could have an additional column on it for recording this figure from each sales check. Alternatively, the number of guests can be arrived at by running an adding machine total or mentally adding the figures from the sales checks.

Comparisons of average check figures can be made from day to day, from week to week, or from month to month, in order to detect a trend. A reduction of the average check over a period of time is not desirable, so efforts should then be made to reverse the trend by advertising, promotion, or improved service. However, a reduced average check combined with a more than proportionate increase in customers can sometimes be advantageous. All other costs being equal during a month, it would be better to have 10,000 customers each spending $1.95 than 9,000 each spending $2:

$$10,000 \times \$1.95 = \$19,500$$
$$9,000 \times \$2.00 = \$18,000$$

The assumption would also have to be made in this illustration that the increased number of customers will get the same level of service as would the lesser number.

### Separating Tax

If tax is assessed on food or beverage items and if this tax is *included* in the selling price that appears on the food menu

| | | TODAY | | | THIS YEAR | | M.T.D. | LAST YEAR | | M.T.D. |
|---|---|---|---|---|---|---|---|---|---|---|
| AVERAGE FOOD CHECK PER ROOM | | | | | | | | | | |
| DAY | | | | DATE | | | | | | |
| | | FOOD SALES | COVERS | AVER. CHECK | FOOD SALES | COVERS | AVER. CHECK | FOOD SALES | COVERS | AVER. CHECK |
| Monday | B | | | | | | | | | |
| | L | | | | | | | | | |
| | D | | | | | | | | | |
| | T | | | | | | | | | |
| Tuesday | B | | | | | | | | | |
| | L | | | | | | | | | |
| | D | | | | | | | | | |
| | T | | | | | | | | | |
| Wednesday | B | | | | | | | | | |
| | L | | | | | | | | | |
| | D | | | | | | | | | |
| | T | | | | | | | | | |
| Thursday | B | | | | | | | | | |
| | L | | | | | | | | | |
| | D | | | | | | | | | |
| | T | | | | | | | | | |
| Friday | B | | | | | | | | | |
| | L | | | | | | | | | |
| | D | | | | | | | | | |
| | T | | | | | | | | | |
| Saturday | B | | | | | | | | | |
| | L | | | | | | | | | |
| | D | | | | | | | | | |
| | T | | | | | | | | | |
| Sunday | B | | | | | | | | | |
| | L | | | | | | | | | |
| | D | | | | | | | | | |
| | T | | | | | | | | | |
| GRAND TOTAL | | | | | | | | | | |

**Figure 2.11** Illustration of type of form that could be used for summarizing and analyzing average check information.

or drink list, it should be excluded when calculating the average check. The simplest method of doing this is to add the percentage of tax to 100, divide this figure into total revenue (which includes tax), and multiply by 100. The answer arrived at will be total (net) sales, from which the average check can then be calculated. Suppose the tax rate is 5 percent; our equation would be

$$\text{Total (net) sales} = \frac{\text{Total revenue (incl. tax)}}{(100 + 5)} \times 100$$

If revenue totaled $21,000 including a 5 percent tax

$$\text{Total (net) sales} = \frac{\$21,000}{105} \times 100 = \$20,000$$

The result obtained can readily be verified, as follows:

| | |
|---|---:|
| Total (net) sales | $ 20,000 |
| 5% x $20,000 (tax) | 1,000 |
| Total revenue (incl. tax) | $ 21,000 |

## BANQUET SALES CONTROL

Because banquets and related functions (wedding receptions, cocktail parties) are quite different in nature from the day-to-day food service in a dining room or coffee shop, control over banquet sales is discussed separately in this section. The following four basic records will generally ensure good control over banquet sales:

1. Daily banquet diary
2. Banquet contract form
3. Weekly banquet sheet
4. Sales check/billing form

Each of these will be discussed in turn.

### Daily Banquet Diary

The daily banquet diary (see Figure 2.13) is the starting point for all functions. As soon as banquet sales personnel make contact with a potential client or organization, the necessary information is entered on the appropriate page of the diary (which usually has one page for each day of the year). The initial entry is made in pencil to indicate that the booking is still tentative. Only when it has been confirmed and a deposit made and/or the banquet contract form (Figure 2.14) signed is the entry completed in ink or ballpoint pen.

The daily banquet diary is the source of all information concerning a function. Once a banquet contract form has been

**Figure 2.12** Banquets and similar functions require some special controls. Photograph courtesy Hotel Vancouver, Vancouver, B.C.

| DAILY BANQUET DIARY | | | | | | | |
|---|---|---|---|---|---|---|---|
| *Monday April 5* | | | | | | | |
| Room | | Time | Estimated Number | Name, Address, Phone | Type of Function | Price | Details |
| Ballroom | A. M. | | | | | | |
| | P. M. | 6.30 | 250 | *Construction Assoc.*<br>*7575 Main St*<br>*681-7098 (Mr. Miles)* | *Banquet* | *$5.75* | *Bar 6.30*<br>*Dinner 7.30* |
| North Room | A. M. | 11.45 | 75 | *Rotary Club*<br>*747-3148 (Mr. Kingsky)* | *Club Lunch* | *$3.50* | *No extras* |
| | P. M. | | | | | | |
| South Room | A. M. | 12 noon | 25 | *Alliance Inc.*<br>*1560 Grange St*<br>*461-1616 (Mr. Jones)* | *Meeting* | *$50.00* | *Will be given later* |
| | P. M. | | | | | | |

**Figure 2.13** The daily banquet diary is the initial record used for control of banquet and related functions sales. In it are listed both tentative and definite bookings.

```
┌─────────────────────────────────────────────────────────────────────┐
│                    BANQUET CONTRACT FORM                    #6321     │
├─────────────────────────────────────────────────────────────────────┤
│ Type of Function    Banquet                                          │
├─────────────────────────────────────────────────────────────────────┤
│ Date and Day   Monday April 5    Time  6.30 pm.   Room  Ballroom     │
├─────────────────────────────────────────────────────────────────────┤
│ Name of Organization    Construction Association                     │
├─────────────────────────────────────────────────────────────────────┤
│ Address        7575 Main St.                  Phone   681-7098       │
├─────────────────────────────────────────────────────────────────────┤
│ Name of Representative   Mr. Miles                                   │
├─────────────────────────────────────────────────────────────────────┤
│ Address            as above                   Phone                  │
├─────────────────────────────────────────────────────────────────────┤
│ Meeting Room Rent $      /        Cash Deposit $   not required      │
├─────────────────────────────────────────────────────────────────────┤
│ Price (per person) $  5.75   No. Expected  250   No. Guaranteed 225  │
├─────────────────────────────────────────────────────────────────────┤
│ Comments   Bar 6.30   Dinner 7.30                                   │
└─────────────────────────────────────────────────────────────────────┘
```

| MENU | WINES |
|---|---|
| Consome Royale | |
| Broiled Half Chicken | |
| Creamed Potatoes | SPECIAL DETAILS |
| Carrots Vichy | Cash Bar $1.00 / drink |
| Neopolitan Ice Cream | |
| Coffee | Add gratuity 15% to food bill |

Approved by Client  A. J. Miles.                    Date  March 3

Distribution:  Banquet Manager
               Chef
               Purchasing Office
               Accounting Office

**Figure 2.14** The banquet contract form is signed by the client when all details have been finalized for a future function. Copies are then distributed to the various departments or employees involved.

signed, that document will contain all the relevent information from the daily banquet diary plus additional information that will allow more detailed planning of the actual banquet. An important consideration (in order to maximize revenue) is to set a deadline for each tentative booking by which banquet sales personnel will have contacted the person who made it to confirm or cancel. This deadline could be as much as two months prior to the date booked. In this way the booking can be confirmed and the banquet contract form signed, or the booking canceled and the space released for some other possible function.

### Banquet Contract Form

The banquet contract form (Figure 2.14) should be designed in such a way that it contains not only the basic information from the daily banquet diary, but also additional information, such as, the actual menu. Copies of this document can then be distributed to all those involved in the banquet. The client, obviously, will receive a copy; other copies will be required by the purchaser, so that food and other items can be ordered (see Chapter 3); the chef, so that he can plan his production requirements; the banquet manager, for setup and staffing purposes; and the accounting office, for billing and control purposes.

One item on this form should be discussed – the *guarantee*. Most clients booking banquets are required to give a guarantee that they will pay for a minimum number of covers if the banquet is not fully attended. For example, if a function is booked for 200 persons with a guarantee of 175, and only 150 people attend, the client will be billed for 175. If more than 175 attend, the client will be billed for the actual number. Most hotels or restaurants with banquet facilities are flexible with this policy, however. Despite the contract, they will check with the client twenty-four hours or more prior to the event for a last-minute estimate of the number of guests expected. If necessary, the guarantee limit can then be lowered, and the hotel or restaurant is protected from overproduction and overpurchasing.

The completed banquet contract forms are best filed in a ring binder or file box, chronologically by date of actual banquet. They should be kept in the office that handles bookings.

### Weekly Banquet Sheet

A few days prior to each week's business, the banquet department should prepare a weekly banquet sheet from the banquet contract forms for banquets to be held that week. The

| FUNCTION | | DAY AND DATE | |
|---|---|---|---|
| TIME | | PRICE PER PERSON | ROOM CHARGE / GUARANTEE |
| ROOM | | **ROOM SET UP** | |
| PREPARE FOR | | TH ☐ | |
| COMPANY | | SCH. R. ☐ | |
| ADDRESS | CITY | RDS. ☐ | |
| CONTACT | TELEPHONE | B.R. ☐ | |
| SPECIAL BILLING INSTRUCTIONS | | U ☐ | |
| | | OTHER ☐ | |
| **MENU** | | HT ☐  ELEV. ☐ | |
| | | T. NO. ☐ | |
| | | SEAT PLAN ☐ | |
| | | WE COLL. TICK. ☐  THEY ☐ | |
| | | LECTERN ☐ | |
| | | EASEL ☐ | |
| | | BLACKB. ☐ | |
| | | FLOWERS ☐ | |
| | | CANDLES ☐ | |
| | | CANDALABRA ☐ | |
| | | PROJECTION ☐ | |
| | | PROJ. EQT. ☐ | |
| | | LIGHTING ☐ | |
| BAR REQUIREMENTS | | ORCHESTRA ☐ | |
| | | PLATFORM ☐ | |
| REMARKS | | PIANO ☐ | |
| | | FLAGS ☐ | |
| | | FAVOURS ☐ | |
| GUARANTEES ON ALL FOOD FUNCTIONS ARE REQUESTED 48 HOURS PRIOR TO THE FUNCTION | | MISC. ☐ | |
| HOTEL SIGNATURE | | GUEST SIGNATURE | |

IF ABOVE ARRANGEMENTS ARE SATISFACTORY PLEASE SIGN ONE COPY AND RETURN

**Figure 2.15** Sample of a typical banquet contract form.

weekly banquet sheet (Figure 2.16) is simply a summary of the more pertinent information about each banquet. Copies of this form are distributed to the same people who receive copies of the banquet contract form so that they can have, at a glance, a complete listing of all upcoming functions week by week. In a hotel, copies of this weekly banquet sheet would also be distributed to the general manager, the bar manager, the executive housekeeper, and the front office manager.

| WEEKLY BANQUET SHEET | | | | | | | Week of | _April 5-11_ | |
|---|---|---|---|---|---|---|---|---|---|
| Day | Month | Date | Room | Organization | Time | Type of Function | Est. No. | Price | |
| Monday | April | 5 | Ballroom | Constr. Assoc. | 6.30 7.30 | Bar Dinner | 250 | 5.75 | |
| | | | North Room | Rotary | 11.45 | Lunch | 75 | 3.50 | |
| | | | South Room | Alliance Inc. | noon | Meeting | 25 | 50.00 | |
| | | | | | | | | | |
| | | | | | | | | | |
| Tuesday | April | 6 | Ballroom | Pace Co. | noon | Lunch | 340 | 4.25 | |
| | | | Ballroom | Western Group | 7.00 | Dinner | 320 | 6.50 | |
| | | | West Room | Mr. Archer | 11.30 | Lunch | 15 | 4.25 | |

**Figure 2.16** The weekly banquet sheet, prepared in advance, gives employees concerned a complete listing, with all pertinent details, of all banquets for the forthcoming week.

### Sales Check/Billing Form

Immediately after each banquet, the head waiter or other responsible person will complete a sales check/billing form. This form can be similar to the basic sales check (Figure 2.3), but in most cases probably needs to be more comprehensive (see Figure 2.17). Certain information will be filled in by the head waiter (number of people served), but much of the information will be completed by the accounting office after certain other control forms have been checked (the banquet control form, Figure 8.9, and the banquet liquor control form, Figure 10.9). Accounting office personnel will also have to check the banquet contract form for certain other information, with particular reference to the amount of deposit and the minimum guarantee.

Although larger establishments may use more, and more sophisticated, forms than those explained and illustrated, the use of these four basic records by even quite small operations should ensure that revenue is maximized and costs controlled.

### SUMMARY

To have good control over sales, sales checks listing what has been sold to each customer or party of customers are required. However, there may be circumstances in which the use of sales checks is not practical — for example, in cafeterias.

| SALES CHECK/BILLING FORM | | | |
|---|---|---|---|
| Organization | *Construction Association* | | |
|  | *7575 Main St.* | | |
| Date *April 5* | Contract No. *6321* | | |
| FOOD | | $ | ¢ |
| _241_ covers @ _5.75_ | | *1385.* | *75* |
| BEVERAGE | | | |
| _____ drinks @ _____ | | | |
| MEETING ROOM RENT | | | |
| OTHER CHARGES _____ | | | |
|  | | | |
| TAX | | | |
| GRATUITIES *15 %* | | *207.* | *85* |
| TOTAL CHARGES | | *1593.* | *60* |
| Less Deposit | | | |
| NET AMOUNT | | *1593.* | *60* |

**Figure 2.17** Sample of a type of sales check that could be used for recording revenue from each separate function.

There are two basic approaches to control of sales, manual systems or machine systems. The *manual system* requires

1. Sequentially prenumbered sales checks
2. Duplicates for ordering food from the kitchen and beverages from the bar
3. Control of the issuance and use of sales checks and duplicates
4. A manual listing (summary) of sales on journal sheets

With a manual system, the control office has to do a considerable amount of checking each day, including:

1. Spot-checking prices, extensions, and additions handwritten on the sales checks

| | | | MEALS SERVED | PRICE | AMOUNT |
|---|---|---|---|---|---|

CHEF BANQUET CONTROL

CHEF _____    DATE_____

| NAME | ROOM | FUNCTION | MEALS SERVED | PRICE | AMOUNT |
|---|---|---|---|---|---|
| | | | | | |
| | | | | | |
| | | | | | |
| | | | | | |
| | | | | | |
| | | | | | |
| | | | | | |
| | | | | | |
| | | | | | |

**Figure 2.18** Type of form that could be completed by chef to summarize information about each banquet.

2. Ensuring that sales checks are properly "summarized" on the sales check journal sheets or on adding machine tapes

3. Adding journal sheet column totals

4. Balancing cash to journal sheet total or adding machine total

5. Ensuring that there are no missing sales checks

Much of the paperwork and effort can be avoided by using machines. Machine systems considerably reduce the amount of documentation required; sales checks do not need to be numbered and therefore no control over their issuance is necessary. No duplicates, either for food or for bar items, are necessary. The machine issues its own duplicate as the sale is rung up on the sales check (thus the term *precheck* to describe the machine). No journal sheets are required; the machine prints out totals each shift or day of total sales by type of item, and total sales for each separate waiter or waitress. Cashiers are not required, as each waiter or waitress can act as his or her own cashier, remitting cash at the end of each shift to correspond to the machine total, adjusted for corrections and/or charge sales.

The basic machine is called the *precheck*. A more sophisticated model is called the *preset precheck*. The main difference between the two is that the latter machine is programed (preset) with prices to correspond with each menu item, up to a total of thirty-six. In this way there can be no pricing errors on sales checks, unless some menu items do not have their prices preset and have to be rung up in the regular way. Prices can be quickly and easily reset in the machine.

The newest development is the electronic register, which operates on the same principle as the preset precheck machines, but is a lot faster and has a much greater capacity. It includes a memory unit for storing information about menu prices, price changes, detailed sales data, and even inventory data.

The average check statistic can be useful for detecting trends of increasing or declining guest spending. It is calculated using the following equation:

$$\text{Average check} = \frac{\text{Total sales}}{\text{Number of guests}}$$

If tax is included in the sales figures, it should be taken out in order to obtain total (net) sales for calculating the average check:

$$\text{Total (net) sales} = \frac{\text{Total revenue (incl. tax)}}{(100 + \text{percent tax})} \times 100$$

Banquet and related function sales generally have to be handled differently from the normal day-to-day sales of food and beverages. Each function is a separate, unique, and often highly specialized transaction, and its control from initial booking through final serving requires some specialized forms. Four were discussed in this chapter: daily banquet diary, banquet contract form, weekly banquet sheet, and the sales check/billing form. The use of these four basic forms should ensure no loss of revenue and good control over costs.

## DISCUSSION QUESTIONS

1. Why are sales checks useful in food and beverage control?

2. What *basic* information appears on sales checks?

3. What purposes do duplicates of sales checks serve?

4. Why is it important to have control over blank sales checks issued?

5. Describe how a sales check journal sheet is used.

6. What five steps are carried out daily by the control office with a manual system of control in effect?

7. Describe briefly how a precheck machine system operates.

8. What is the difference between a precheck machine and a preset precheck machine?

9. How is the average check calculated and of what use is it to management?

10. Briefly describe the use of four basic forms that will aid in banquet control.


## MULTIPLE CHOICE/DISCUSSION QUESTIONS

1. Which of the following would *not* be a requirement for good internal control of sales

   a. A forecast each day of the anticipated sales.
   b. Qualified and trained cashiers.
   c. Controlling the issuing of unused sales checks.
   d. Verifying each day that there are no missing sales checks.
   e. Spot-checking prices, extensions, and additions on sales checks.

2. If a dining room uses a system of handwritten sales checks (manual system) with payment made by the guest to the waiter, who in turn gives the sales check and cash to the cashier, and if on a particular day a sales check is missing you could assume that

   a. The waiter is responsible.
   b. The cashier is responsible.
   c. They are working in collusion and are both responsible.
   d. The guest walked out with the check, without paying.
   e. None of the above is necessarily true.

3. If, with a manual system of sales control, kitchen order duplicates are verified each day for missing numbers and none are missing, can you take it for granted that

   a. There will also be no missing original sales checks.

b. Everything listed on the kitchen duplicate will also be recorded on the corresponding original.

c. Prices, extensions, and additions on originals are all correct.

d. All original sales checks have been properly recorded on the sales check journal sheet.

e. None of the above is necessarily the case.

## PROBLEMS

1. a. The Top of the Tower Restaurant had total food sales (no tax included) during the month of December of $43,250. During this period, 15,120 guests were served. What was the average food check?

   b. During January, this same restaurant served 16,750 guests with an average check of $2.75. All other things being equal, would this be a desirable trend?

   c. The following month, in February, the average check was $2.50 and the number of customers increased again to 17,140. What comment could be made about this new situation?

2. a. The cocktail bar of the Top of the Tower Restaurant had beverage sales during December of $15,160 *including* a 6 percent tax. Calculate the total (net) sales.

   b. In January the tax rate on beverage sales was increased to 8 percent. Beverage sales during January were $16,144, and in February, $14,199. For each of the two months calculate the total (net) sales.

3. The following sales check journal sheet was completed by a dining room cashier (Figure 2.19). Sales checks were turned in with this report, as was cash corresponding with the amount in the Total column. On this particular day there were no charge sales.

   *Required:* a. "Audit" this sheet insofar as is possible with the given information and explain what action you might take about each of the "errors" that you find.

   b. The beverage column total includes a 5 percent tax. Calculate total (net) sales of beverages.

   c. Calculate the *total* average check after making any necessary adjustments called for in (a) and (b) above.

4. You have the sales check journal sheets (separate ones for cash and

| SALES CHECK JOURNAL SHEET | | | Date _March 3_ | Cashier : _C_ | |
|---|---|---|---|---|---|
| Waiter # | Check # | # of Guests | Food | Beverage | Total |
| 3 | 2543 | 6 | 24.10 | | 24.10 |
| 5 | 2779 | 2 | 8.20 | 2.20 | 10.40 |
| 3 | 2544 | 4 | 11.20 | 2.10 | 13.30 |
| 4 | 3015 | 2 | 8.— | | 8.— |
| 5 | 2781 | 4 | 12.90 | | 12.90 |
| 6 | 3214 | 6 | 28.10 | 12.90 | 41.00 |
| 4 | 3016 | 8 | 41.20 | 14.20 | 54.40 |
| 3 | 2547 | 4 | 12.30 | 7.18 | 19.48 |
| 6 | 3216 | 2 | 5.20 | 2.10 | 7.30 |
| 4 | 3012 | 2 | 7.10 | 1.50 | 8.60 |
| 4 | 3014 | 4 | 10.20 | 4.73 | 14.93 |
| 3 | 2545 | 1 | 2.10 | 4.70 | 6.80 |
| 6 | 3215 | 4 | 9.95 | | 9.95 |
| 5 | 2780 | 6 | 31.05 | 9.18 | 41.23 |
| 5 | 2784 | 1 | 3.75 | 0.50 | 4.25 |
| 3 | 2546 | 2 | 4.— | 1.25 | 5.25 |
| 4 | 3013 | 1 | 3.— | 0.85 | 3.85 |
| 3 | 2550 | 2 | 7.20 | 4.— | 11.20 |
| 5 | 2783 | 2 | 8.10 | | 8.10 |
| 3 | 2549 | 1 | 4.30 | 2.10 | 6.40 |
| 4 | 3017 | 1 | 4.05 | 0.50 | 4.55 |
| 4 | 3020 | 4 | 10.05 | 4.82 | 14.87 |
| 3 | 2548 | 2 | 3.90 | 1.00 | 4.90 |
| 5 | 2785 | 3 | 10.50 | 4.70 | 14.20 |
| 4 | 3018 | 1 | 4.05 | 0.50 | 4.55 |
| | | | | | |
| TOTALS | | 75 | 263.50 | 81.01 | 344.51 |

Figure 2.19 Sales check journal sheet

| Date _Nov. 1_ | | | | | SALES CHECK JOURNAL SHEET – CASH | | | | |
| Cashier _Janet_ | Shift _11-3_ | | | | | | | | |
|---|---|---|---|---|---|---|---|---|---|
| Check # | Waiter # | Food | Bev. | Total | Check # | Waiter # | Food | .Bev. | Total |
| 3651 | 3 | 1.75 | 0.60 | 2.35 | Balance Forward | | 178.05 | 34.00 | 210.05 |
| 3996 | 4 | 4.10 | | 4.10 | 4005 | 4 | 1.75 | 0.65 | 2.40 |
| 4022 | 2 | 2.05 | | 2.05 | 4033 | 2 | 9.10 | | 9.10 |
| 3653 | 3 | 17.25 | 2.50 | 15.75 | 4325 | 9 | 0.75 | | 0.75 |
| 3652 | 3 | 6.10 | 1.35 | 7.45 | 4007 | 4 | 1.75 | 0.65 | 2.40 |
| 4021 | 2 | 0.75 | 0.60 | 1.35 | 4327 | 9 | 17.40 | 3.90 | 22.30 |
| 3999 | 4 | 19.95 | | 19.95 | 4328 | 9 | 4.00 | 1.60 | 5.60 |
| 3655 | 3 | 2.30 | 0.80 | 3.10 | 4032 | 2 | 10.00 | 3.90 | 13.90 |
| 3872 | 8 | 9.05 | | 9.05 | 4329 | 9 | 1.75 | | 1.75 |
| 3871 | 8 | 1.45 | | 1.45 | 4008 | 4 | 4.05 | 0.75 | 4.80 |
| 4025 | 2 | 7.30 | 1.30 | 8.60 | 4009 | 4 | 3.20 | | 3.20 |
| 3657 | 3 | 21.45 | 6.95 | 27.40 | 4331 | 9 | 4.60 | 3.10 | 7.70 |
| 3874 | 8 | 0.90 | | 0.90 | 4031 | 2 | 5.00 | 4.95 | 9.95 |
| 4002 | 4 | 1.95 | 0.95 | 2.90 | 4332 | 9 | 9.95 | 2.95 | 13.90 |
| 4319 | 9 | 1.05 | 1.35 | 2.40 | 3876 | 8 | 12.75 | 4.30 | 17.05 |
| 3659 | 3 | 4.00 | | 4.00 | 3881 | 8 | 6.40 | | 6.40 |
| 4322 | 9 | 6.30 | | 6.30 | 4012 | 4 | 1.75 | | 1.75 |
| 4026 | 2 | 1.75 | | 1.75 | 4333 | 9 | 1.75 | 0.65 | 2.40 |
| 3875 | 8 | 0.95 | | 0.95 | 4013 | 4 | 2.80 | | 2.80 |
| 3998 | 4 | 1.85 | 0.65 | 2.50 | 4334 | 9 | 1.75 | 0.65 | 2.40 |
| ~~3658~~ | ~~3~~ | ~~17.00~~ | ~~1.95~~ | ~~18.95~~ | 3877 | 8 | 4.35 | 1.20 | 5.55 |
| 3997 | 4 | 8.10 | 0.90 | 9.00 | 3878 | 8 | 1.05 | | 1.05 |
| 4321 | 9 | 4.35 | | 4.35 | 4335 | 9 | 3.90 | 1.30 | 5.20 |
| 4027 | 2 | 1.75 | .65 | 2.40 | 3880 | 8 | 1.05 | | 1.05 |
| 4028 | 2 | 1.75 | .65 | 2.40 | 4015 | 4 | 3.70 | 1.30 | 5.00 |
| 4003 | 4 | 1.95 | | 1.95 | ~~3881~~ | ~~8~~ | ~~6.40~~ | | ~~6.40~~ |
| 4324 | 9 | 17.20 | 6.90 | 24.10 | 4014 | 4 | 21.40 | 14.70 | 36.10 |
| 4006 | 4 | 8.30 | 5.60 | 13.90 | | | | | |
| 4323 | 9 | 1.25 | 0.65 | 1.90 | | | | | |
| 4004 | 4 | 6.05 | | 6.05 | | | | | |
| 4030 | 2 | 14.10 | | 14.10 | | | | | |
| 4328 | 9 | 4.00 | 1.60 | 5.60 | Totals | | 304.00 | 80.55 | 384.55 |
| Balance Forward | | 178.05 | 34.00 | 210.05 | Cash Remitted | | | | 365.05 |

Figure 2.20 Sales check journal sheet — cash

Date _November 1_      SALES CHECK JOURNAL SHEET - CHARGE

Cashier _Janet_   Shift _11-3_

| Check # | Waiter # | Food | Beverage | Grat. | Total | Name | Room # | Cr. Card # |
|---------|----------|------|----------|-------|-------|------|--------|------------|
| 3654 | 3 | 1.75 | .65 | .25 | 2.65 | HARVEY | 401 | |
| 3995 | 4 | 3.95 | | | 3.95 | WOOLTON | 324 | |
| 4001 | 4 | 6.20 | 2.10 | 1.00 | 9.30 | CRASKI | | Amexco 400 602 719 |
| 3658 | 3 | 17.00 | 1.95 | | 18.95 | SMITH | | Shell 103 401 206 |
| 4010 | 4 | 1.30 | | | 1.30 | MOLONEY | 145 | |
| 3873 | 8 | 2.90 | 5.40 | .10 | 8.40 | PUGH | | Diners 627 094 9A |
| ~~3876~~ | ~~8~~ | ~~12.75~~ | ~~4.30~~ | | ~~17.05~~ | | | |
| 4023 | 2 | 2.10 | | .25 | 2.35 | FALEY | | Diners 600 043 78 |
| 4011 | 4 | 4.90 | 2.10 | | 7.00 | CRIMP | 430 | |
| 4024 | 2 | 24.00 | 6.50 | 3.50 | 34.00 | NIXON | | Amexco H09 411 722 |
| 3879 | 8 | .75 | .90 | .20 | 1.85 | DROOL | 190 | |
| 4320 | 9 | 2.45 | .60 | | 3.05 | KOHL | | Carte Blanche 42-075C |
| 4029 | 2 | 9.35 | 2.10 | | 11.45 | TANGY | 105 | |
| 4326 | 9 | 1.75 | .60 | .25 | 2.60 | TISH | 210 | |
| 4330 | 9 | 1.75 | .60 | .25 | 2.60 | TOSH | 211 | |
| | | | | | | | | |
| | | | | | | | | |
| | | | | | | | | |
| | | | | | | | | |
| | | | | | | | | |
| | | | | | | | | |
| | | | | | | | | |
| | | | | | | | | |
| | | | | | | | | |
| | | | | | | | | |
| | | | | | | | | |
| TOTALS | | 80.15 | 23.50 | 5.80 | 109.45 | | | |

Figure 2.21 Sales check journal sheet—charge

charge sales) for a hotel's dining room luncheon period on November 1 (Figures 2.20 and 2.21). The cashier has reported (as you can see from the bottom right-hand side of the cash journal sheet) that she is short $19.50 in her cash.

On going through the sales checks for that day, you notice that the signature of Mr. Kolowski, and a guest room number, appear on the back of 4032. The check is listed on the cash journal sheet. You confirm that Mr. Kolowski is still registered in the hotel. This error must be corrected.

From your sales check list you know that the numbers of the last checks used on October 31 were 4020, 3650, 3993, 3870, and 4318.

Audit these journal sheets insofar as is possible with the given information, listing all mistakes discovered and making a brief comment about what action you would take, if any, about each of them.

# 3

# Food Purchasing

## Objectives

After studying this chapter, the reader will be able to

1. Define in a sentence or two some of the more common terms used in food purchasing, such as "specifications," "standing orders," "blind receiving."

2. Describe procedures and forms that will help in controlling food costs and reducing losses.

Those involved in purchasing food must know the market and be familiar with market trends. They must also be aware of new products as they are introduced, and of external factors (weather, transportation problems) that could alter current market prices.

## FOOD ORDERING

### Specifications

It is preferable, where the size of operation permits, for specifications to be prepared for meat, fish, poultry, and dry goods. These specifications can be prepared by the control department in conjunction with the chef and the food and beverage manager. For meat, for example, they should contain such items as quality or grade, weight, degree of aging, amount of fat, and cutting instructions. Similar specifications should be prepared for all products purchased. Specification sheets are drawn up in triplicate—one copy for the supplier (s), one copy for the person responsible for receiving goods, one copy for the control office. Such specifications are usually used, as stated, for meat, fish, poultry, and dry goods bought in relatively large quantities or in case lots, on a weekly or monthly basis (Figure 3.1).

FOOD SPECIFICATIONS

Company ___*J.J. Joseph*___

Address ___*1234 Main*___          Phone ___*681-7098*___

Effective ___*Oct. 1*___     through ___*Dec. 31*___

Item ___*Beef Ribs*___

| Specifications | Price |
|---|---|
| *Choice* | *$1.85 max.* |
| *7 Ribs* | |
| *10 inch Flank Trim* | |
| *35-37 lbs.* | |
| | |
| | |
| | |

**Figure 3.1** A completed specification form.

### Daily Purchases

For perishable items purchased on a daily basis, such as dairy and bakery goods, and fresh fruits and vegetables, a *par stock* limit could be set for each item. The par stock would be the quantity that should be on hand at the beginning of each day to take care of that day's business.

What is to be ordered each day is the quantity that would bring the amount on hand for each item up to its par stock level. A useful control form to aid in this is illustrated in Figure 3.2. This control form is useful for "normal" day-to-day requirements. If additional quantities of any item are required for special days or functions, the person who does the ordering would have to be notified. This form must be completed early in the morning so that orders can be given to suppliers for same-day delivery.

### Standing Orders

In some operations, standing orders are left with suppliers to eliminate some of the daily inventory taking, form completing, and ordering. Standing orders direct suppliers to deliver specified

| DAILY PURCHASE SHEET | | | Date _Oct. 1_ | |
|---|---|---|---|---|
| Item | Size | Par Stock | On Hand | Required |
| FRUIT - Apples, Golden Del. | 138 & 1gr. | 3 cases | *1+* | *2* |
| Apples, Newton | 120's | 3 cases | *1 3/4* | *1* |
| Avocados | 40 - 48's | 1 case - | *0* | *1* |
| Bananas, Chiquita | 20# | 40 lb. | *18 lb.* | *20 lb.* |
| Grapefruit, White | 32's | 4 cases | *2+* | *2* |
| Grapefruit, Red | 48's | 5 cases | *1 -* | *4* |
| | | | | |

**Figure 3.2** The daily purchase sheet is useful for listing requirements to bring present inventory up to par for each day's anticipated volume.

quantities of particular perishables without the steward or purchasing agent having to call in the order daily. Such orders can be changed to meet changing needs.

### Food Tests

All products should be tested before they are purchased. As new products appear on the market, they too should be tested. The results of the tests can be incorporated into the purchasing specifications.

*Canned food* tests serve to ensure that the best net weight yield is achieved after the liquid in which the food is packed has been drained. They can also be used to verify the count, quality, and uniformity of the contents, and even the quality of the syrup or juice in which the ingredients are packed. *Fruit and vegetable* tests ensure that the best count or weight is received for money spent. *Cooking, trim and butchering* tests are necessary in the case of meat, poultry, and fish. These tests will be discussed in detail in Chapter 7.

## WHO DOES THE ORDERING?

In a large operation, a purchasing department would do the ordering; in a smaller operation, it could be the steward or storekeeper. In a very small operation, it might even be the chef.

| ON HAND | AMT. | UNIT | PACK | SPECIFICATIONS | DELIVERY DATE | RECIPIENT DEALER | PRICE | CHECK |
|---|---|---|---|---|---|---|---|---|
| DATE _____ | | | | | | NUMBER _____ | | |
| | | | | | | | | |
| | | | | | | | | |
| | | | | | | | | |
| | | | | | | | | |
| | | | | | | | | |
| | | | | | | | | |
| | | | | | | | | |
| | | | | | | | | |
| | | | | | | | | |
| | | | | | | | | |
| | | | | | | | | |
| | | | | | | | | |
| | | | | | | | | |
| | | | | | | | | |
| | | | | | | | | |
| | | | | | | | | |
| | | | | | | | | |
| | | | | | | | | |
| | | | | | | | | |
| | | | | | | | | |
| | | | | | | | | |
| | | | | | | | | |
| | | | | | | | | |
| | | | | | | | | |
| | | | | | | | | |
| | | | | | | | | |
| | | | | | | | | |

REMARKS _____  _____

APPROVED SIGNATURE_____

UNDER SPECIFICATIONS LIST ALL PERTINENT DATA, I.E. : GRADE, BRAND, COUNT, GRAVITY, SIEVE, HEAVY OR LIGHT SYRUP, OR DRY PACK, PEELED OR UNPEELED; WHOLE, HALVES, SLICED, ETC.

**Figure 3.3** Illustration of a combined daily purchase sheet and food specifications form.

Whoever does the ordering should buy from the supplier who can provide the quality desired at the lowest price. In the case of meat, poultry, fish, and other items for which specifications have been prepared, the supplier must be instructed to adhere to these specifications. It is recommended that at least two quotations for each item be received. Figure 3.4 shows a useful form for recording market quotations.

## Order Form (Order Book)

Whatever the circumstances and whatever the size of the operation, one item is indispensable: a food order book or form, which is completed by the person who actually does the ordering. It contains the date the order was made, the supplier's name, a brief description of the food ordered, the quantity ordered, the price quoted by the supplier, and the date of delivery (filled in later). An additional column for comments (such as short order, back order, returned because of poor quality, etc.) will be found useful. An example of such a form is shown in Figure 3.7.

An alternative to this form, and one that is probably more useful in high volume establishments, is a preprinted sheet listing all items normally carried in stock. A sample of this type of order sheet is shown in Figure 3.8. Its advantage is that it considerably reduces the amount of writing required. The receiver should have the order book or form on hand when goods are received so that he can be sure that what has been ordered is received, and that quantities ordered and prices quoted match the invoices delivered with the goods.

| MARKET QUOTATION SHEET | | Date _Oct. 1_ | | |
|---|---|---|---|---|
| Item | Required | Quotations | | |
| | | J.J. Joseph | Mid West | Hinton |
| BEEF – Corned | 5 lb. | 1.10 | 1.03 | 1.07 |
| Butt | | | | |
| Chuck | | | | |
| Filet | 8 lb. | 3.10 | 3.05 | 3.25 |
| Short Loin | | | | |
| Ribs | 35 lb. | 1.83 | 1.85 | 1.90 |
| | | | | |

**Figure 3.4** At least two quotes should be received for each separate item required. The market quotation sheet, completed daily, is useful for summarizing requirements and quotations.

| Order Date | | | Delivery Date | | |
|---|---|---|---|---|---|
| **ITEMS** | WANTED | DEALERS | **ITEMS** | WANTED | DEALERS |
| **FRESH FRUIT** | | | **FRESH VEGETABLES** | | |
| Avocados ·30's | | | Artichokes | | |
| Apples · Baking | | | Asparagus crt | | |
| Fruit · Baskets | | | Beans Ky Green | | |
| Bananas · 40 lb ctn | | | " wax | | |
| **Berries —Flats** | | | Beets | | |
| Blackberries · 12's Flat | | | Broccoli Doz | | |
| Blueberries 12's | | | Cabbage, Green crt | | |
| | | | " Red crt | | |
| Raspberries · 12's | | | " Savoy crt | | |
| Strawberries · 12's " | | | Carrots, local (50) sk | | |
| | | | " Calif. (50) sk | | |
| Cherries · Flats | | | Cauliflower, crt | | |
| Chestnuts · Fresh lb. | | | Celery, local crt | | |
| Grapes ·Red 27 lb. | | | " Calif. crt | | |
| " · Green " | | | Corn, Golden Bantam crt | | |
| " · White " | | | Cranberries lb. | | |
| " · Black " | | | Cucumbers, White spine doz. | | |
| Grapefruit · Florida 27 | | | " Long Eng. " | | |
| " " 32 | | | Egg Plant crt | | |
| " " 48 | | | Onion, Spanish lb. | | |
| " Calif. 27 | | | " Jumbo (50) sk | | |
| " " 32 | | | " Med. (50) sk | | |
| " " 48 | | | Parsnips sk | | |
| Lemons · skt 140 | | | Peas, Green sk | | |
| " " 165 | | | **Potatoes** | | |
| Limes · lb | | | Local No. 1 sk | | |
| **Melons** | | | Alta Gems sk | | |
| Canteloupe · 27 crt | | | Idaho Gems sk | | |
| " 36 " | | | Idaho Bakers 100 sk | | |
| " 45 " | | | Spinach (20) crt | | |
| Casaba | | | Squash, Acorn lb. | | |

**Figure 3.5** A daily market quotation sheet used in industry.

**Figure 3.6** Wherever possible, a minimum of two market quotations should be obtained before food orders are placed.

| | | | FOOD ORDERS | | | | | |
|---|---|---|---|---|---|---|---|---|
| Date | Item | Supplier | Quantity | Price | Total | Received | Comments | |
| Oct.1 | Corned Beef | Mid West | 5 | 1.03 | 5.15 | Oct.1 | | |
| | Filet | " " | 8 | 3.05 | 24.40 | " | | |
| | Ribs | Joseph | 35 | 1.83 | 64.05 | " | | |
| | Turkey | " | 75 | 0.89 | 66.75 | " | | |
| | Pork Butt | " | 50 | 0.91½ | 45.75 | " | | |

**Figure 3.7** All food items ordered should be listed on an order form or in an order book. In this way the receiver knows what is coming in and can verify that invoice quantities and prices agree with what is listed on the form or in the book.

FOOD ORDERS   Order date __Oct 1__   Delivery date __Oct 1__

| Item | Order | Price | Supplier | Item | Order | Price | Supplier |
|---|---|---|---|---|---|---|---|
| Beef – Corned | 5 lb. | 1.03 | Mid West | Fruit – Apples, G.D. | 2 cs. | 7.25 | Growers |
| – Butt | | | | – ", Newton | 1 cs. | 7.85 | " |
| – Chuck | | | | – Avocados | 1 cs. | 17.25 | " |
| – Filet | 8 lb. | 3.05 | Mid West | – Bananas, Ch. | 20 lb. | 3.35 | " |
| | | | | | | | |

**Figure 3.8** Having items preprinted on the food order form speeds up the daily process of listing items ordered.

## FOOD DELIVERIES

### Delivery Hours

Suppliers should be instructed to deliver goods between certain specified hours. In large operations where a receiver is on duty full time, these hours could spread between 7 A.M. and 5 P.M. In a very small establishment, where one person combines food receiving with other jobs, deliveries should be made only during the hours that person is available for receiving. In any event, it is obviously important to ensure that deliveries are made only when someone is there to receive them.

### Invoice with Goods

Suppliers should be advised to deliver a fully priced invoice with the goods so that the receiver can check quantities received against quantities invoiced. These invoices also serve other functions which will be explained in Chapters 4 and 5.

### Blind Receiving

Some establishments follow the practice of *blind receiving*. In this case, the supplier is instructed *not* to supply an invoice with the goods, but to mail it directly to the accounting office. With the goods will be a delivery or packing slip that shows no weights or counts, so that the receiver is forced to count or weigh every item received and to record these weights or counts on the delivery slip.

## SUMMARY

A qualified person who knows the market is required to handle the ordering (purchasing) of food items. Specifications should be drawn up for major purchases such as meat, fish, poultry, and dry goods. These items are frequently purchased in large quantities, and usually not on a daily basis. For items purchased daily (primarily perishable items such as fruit, vegetables, dairy, and bakery goods) par stock levels should be set. What is ordered each day is the amount required to bring inventory on hand up to par level. Suppliers may also be given standing orders. This means that they will deliver daily a predetermined quantity without their having to be instructed every day.

Food tests, such as canned food tests, fruit and vegetable tests, and cooking, trim, and butchering tests should be carried out in order to set specifications or to ensure that what is being purchased meets the quality desired. A minimum of two suppliers should be contacted for each item required so that purchases of the quality desired can be made at the lowest possible price.

Each day all items to be ordered should be summarized on an order form or in an order book so that the receiver knows what is arriving, in what quantities, and at what prices. Suppliers should be given limited hours during which deliveries can be made. They should be instructed to supply invoices with goods so that quantities ordered and received and prices quoted can be checked against invoices at the time of delivery.

## DISCUSSION QUESTIONS

1. What is a food specification?

2. Define:
   a. Par stock
   b. Standing orders
   c. Food tests

3. What is the value of a market quotation sheet?

4. What are perishable food items?

5. Why is it useful for an invoice to accompany goods received from a supplier?

6. What is blind receiving?

7. Why is it useful to have a food order book or form?

## MULTIPLE CHOICE/DISCUSSION QUESTIONS

1. Specifications are prepared (in a relatively large food operation) by
   a. The chef.
   b. The food and beverage manager.
   c. Control office personnel.
   d. All the above working together.
   e. None of the above.

2. Delivery hours for food purchases should be specified to the supplier
   a. So that he can schedule his staffing requirements.
   b. In order that he can more readily organize his drivers' delivery routes.
   c. So that nothing will be delivered to the food establishment during hours when there is nobody there to receive them.
   d. So that he can prepare invoices in advance to deliver with the goods.
   e. In order that he can deliver outside those hours, thus obliging the food establishment to practice "blind receiving."

3. It is suggested that two or more quotations be received for each purchase. This is desirable so that

a. Only the lowest-priced supplier will always be the one who receives the order.
b. The suppliers with the higher prices can be telephoned back in order to get them to reduce their quotations.
c. The restaurant has a record of the quotation to ensure that the supplier does not quote a higher price the next time.
d. The average price from all suppliers can be recorded in the order book.
e. Purchases can be made from the supplier who gives the best price consistent with the quality desired.

## PROBLEM

1. You have been appointed food and beverage comptroller of a restaurant complex with a sales volume of approximately $1 million a year. No one has had this job before you, and you find there is no control system presently in effect for the purchasing and ordering of food. Until now the chef has been ordering and purchasing some food items. The storekeeper has been ordering and purchasing others and has been responsible for all receiving. There have been no formal documents or records in use. The manager and the accountant, to whom you report, have explained that the operation has been running at a higher food cost than they think it should.

Write a report to the accountant describing what procedures and forms could be used to aid in reducing and controlling food cost. Do not include samples of the forms, as this is only a preliminary report, but briefly describe the use of any forms and why they would help in cutting food cost. State also who will be responsible for form completion and for carrying out the proposed procedures.

The number of forms should be limited to as few as possible. The procedures should be as simple as possible. The report should be as brief as possible.

# 4

# Receiving
# and
# the Receiving Report

## Objectives

After studying this chapter, the reader will be able to

1. List six common methods by which suppliers and/or delivery drivers can profit from a food operation's lack of good receiving practices.

2. List at least seven standard practices in good food receiving.

3. Differentiate between storeroom purchases and direct purchases.

4. Describe the use of a daily food receiving report.

5. Complete and balance a daily food receiving report from information provided by purchase invoices.

There are many ways in which suppliers and delivery drivers can take advantage of an establishment that does not have good receiving practices. For example:

1. Using excess or moisture-laden packaging to substitute for short weight of actual items.

2. Putting proper quality food on the top level of a packing case and unacceptable quality beneath.

3. Placing items directly in the storeroom or refrigerated areas without the receiver checking them.

4. Supplying short counts or short weights that do not agree with the invoiced quantities.

5. Taking back unsatisfactory merchandise without giving appropriate credit.

6. Invoicing and charging for a higher quality than was actually delivered.

7. Opening cases, removing items, and resealing cases prior to delivery, and charging for full cases on invoices.

Many other "techniques" could be added to this list, but most of them can be overcome by having a set of standard receiving practices and ensuring that they are followed.

## STANDARD PRACTICES

The following should be standard practices in receiving food:

1. Each item that can be counted should be counted.
2. Each item that can be weighed should be weighed (scales must be provided for the receiver).
3. Weights and/or counts should be checked against invoice weights and/or quantities.
4. Quality should be checked ( the  receiver must be knowledgeable about quality).
5. If specifications have been provided, the goods received should be checked against them.
6. Spot-checks of case goods should be made to ensure that cases are full and that the quantity is what it is supposed to be.
7. When an invoice is not received, a memorandum invoice should be prepared by the receiver. On it he can record quantities or weights, descriptions of items, and prices quoted from his market quotation sheet.
8. If goods are short-shipped or if quality is not acceptable, a credit memorandum should be made out by the receiver and signed by the delivery driver, who acknowledges that the goods delivered did not agree with the invoice count or weight, or that he is accepting low-quality food for return to the supplier (Figure 4.1).
9. Invoice prices should be checked against the market quotation sheet (Figure 3.4).

Only when he is entirely satisfied should the receiver sign the delivery driver's copy of the invoice acknowledging receipt of the goods. Because of the high cost of meat, poultry, and fish items, the chef may want to check the quality of these items himself.

### Receiving Stamp

To ensure that the receiver does carry out all required procedures, each invoice should be stamped with a rubber stamp provided for that purpose (Figure 4.4).

| CREDIT MEMORANDUM                    Date _Oct. 1_ |||||
| Supplier ___Atlantic Fishing___ |||||
| Please issue a credit invoice for the following |||||
| Quantity | Item | | Unit Cost | Total |
| 5 lb. | Sole fillets | | $1.30 | $6.50 |
|  |  |  |  |  |
| Reason ___Quality not acceptable___ |||||
| Signature of delivery driver ___C. S. Stacey___ |||||

**Figure 4.1** The credit memorandum is made up by the receiver when goods have to be returned. It is signed by the delivery driver, who takes the duplicate copy back to the supplier as proof that the goods were sent back. The supplier will subsequently issue a credit invoice.

In addition, spot-checks should be carried out by the control office to be sure that the receiver is carrying out all his duties. Complete checking of all deliveries cannot be stressed too much. When a delivery driver notices that weighing scales are not being used or that quantities are not being counted, he may be tempted to short-ship deliveries. If he notices that quality is not being checked, he can substitute a lower quality.

### Distribution

When goods have been fully checked, they should be put as quickly as possible into the appropriate refrigerators or storage areas. Many establishments date-stamp goods on delivery to ensure proper stock rotation. Dry goods (canned goods, cereals, and other items that have a fairly long shelf life) are generally put into a locked storeroom. Perishables (meat, fish, poultry, dairy, and baked goods) are considered as being used up on the day of purchase even though, in fact, this may not be the case; these items are usually referred to as *direct purchases*. A notation must be made by the receiver on each invoice indicating whether the items were distributed to the storeroom or to direct purchases. The need

**Figure 4.2** Weighing scales are a necessity to ensure that the proper weight of goods ordered and invoiced is received. The platform scale on an adjustable wheeled base illustrated here is just one of a variety of models available. Photograph courtesy Toledo Scale Division, Reliance Electric Company, Toledo, Ohio.

**Figure 4.3** Another scale for weighing purchases is the portable utility scale, with readings up to 250 lb. If the dial is obscured by a bulky item, the operator presses a control button below the dial which retains the reading in position. Photograph courtesy Pelouze Scale Company, Evanston, Illinois.

```
┌─────────────────────────────────────────┐
│  Received by_____     │
│  Quantity checked by  _____    │
│  Quality checked by _____    │
│  Prices checked by _____    │
│  Date _____    │
└─────────────────────────────────────────┘
```

**Figure 4.4**

for this notation will become apparent in the next section, in which we discuss the daily food receiving report.

## DAILY FOOD RECEIVING REPORT

At the end of each day the receiver should prepare his daily food receiving report, which summarizes all daily food deliveries to the establishment. To complete the report, each invoice is listed in turn (Figure 4.5), as is the total of the invoice and its distribution to direct purchases, storeroom, or other. As mentioned earlier, if each invoice is stamped "direct purchases" or "stores" on receipt of the goods, it will aid in proper completion of the food receiving report.

| DAILY FOOD RECEIVING REPORT | | Date | Oct. 1 | | | |
|---|---|---|---|---|---|---|
| Supplier | Description | Invoice Total | Direct Purchases | Storeroom | Other |
| Atlantic Fishing | Fresh Fish | 74.29 | 74.29 | | |
| Macdonalds | Dry goods | 142.10 | | 142.10 | |
| Growers | Fruit & Veg. | 61.04 | 57.20 | | 3.84 |
| Mid West | Meat | 29.55 | 29.55 | | |
| III | Meat | 176.55 | 176.55 | | |
| Atlantic Fishing | Fish returned | (6.50) | (6.50) | | |
| | TOTALS | 477.03 | 331.09 | 142.10 | 3.84 |

**Figure 4.5** The daily food receiving report is completed from invoices received with goods purchased and delivered that day.

If an invoice contains some items for direct purchases and some for stores, then it must be appropriately broken down on the receiving report. If goods have been returned and a credit memorandum made out, then these items should show as deductions (see bracketed item on the report illustrated). If an invoice contains items that are neither direct purchases for the food department nor food items for the storeroom, they would be listed in the Other column. An example of this might be fresh eggs purchased specifically for the bar.

When all invoices have been listed, the columns must be added. To aid in ensuring correct addition, the totals of the Direct Purchases, Storeroom, and Other columns should be cross-added to agree with the Total column. In our case, $331.09 + $142.10 + $3.84 = $477.03.

### More Comprehensive Receiving Report

In order to have additional information, larger establishments may wish to have more detail about their purchases. The receiving report then will have columns that allow purchases to be distributed into as many as fifteen categories. At the end of the month, total purchases for each category can be expressed as a percentage of all purchases. Each month these percentages can be compared with the results for the previous month and any change in the pattern of purchases can be immediately identified. For example, let us look at the figures in Table 4.1, which was compiled from information taken from food receiving reports.

As a result of analyzing our purchases in this way, we could assume that the reason for the increase in the food cost percentage for the month of May compared with April was because a greater portion of our purchase dollar went for meat and poultry items—items that may have a lower markup than others on our menu, and thus give a higher food cost percentage. (Food cost and food cost percentage will be discussed in detail in Chapter 7.)

### Receiving Report Summary

The main purpose of the daily food receiving report is to summarize food purchases for that day. However, these daily reports can themselves be summarized each day by transferring

Table 4.1

| Item | April $ | % | May $ | % |
|------|--------|------|--------|------|
| Meat | $ 25,341 | 37.1% | $ 26,754 | 39.4% |
| Poultry | 8,532 | 12.5 | 9,311 | 13.7 |
| Fish | 8,110 | 11.9 | 6,117 | 9.0 |
| Vegetables | 2,276 | 3.3 | 2,195 | 3.2 |
| Fruit | 1,195 | 1.8 | 1,216 | 1.7 |
| Milk | 4,108 | 6.0 | 4,043 | 6.0 |
| Cream | 1,007 | 1.5 | 993 | 1.5 |
| Butter | 3,206 | 4.7 | 3,215 | 4.7 |
| Ice cream | 879 | 1.3 | 919 | 1.4 |
| Eggs | 2,140 | 3.1 | 2,074 | 3.0 |
| Bakery | 7,418 | 10.9 | 7,206 | 10.6 |
| Coffee, tea | 2,111 | 3.1 | 2,143 | 3.2 |
| Cheese | 1,054 | 1.5 | 984 | 1.5 |
| Sundries | 842 | 1.3 | 661 | 1.1 |
| Total cost | $ 68,219 | 100.0% | $ 67,831 | 100.0% |
| Sales | $171,543 | | $165,402 | |
| Food cost % | 39.8% | | 41.0% | |

the column totals to a receiving report summary. This latter form is useful in calculating a daily and a to date food cost percentage, and is an aid in storeroom inventory control (see Chapter 6).

## SUMMARY

The receiving function is an important part of the food cost control process. All incoming goods should be checked to ensure that quantities and/or weights agree with what was ordered and with what is invoiced. Prices quoted should be checked against invoices. Quality should be verified and, where necessary, checked against specifications.

If quality is not up to standard or if goods are being sent back for some other reason, a credit memorandum must be made out by the receiver and signed by the delivery driver who will take the goods back to the supplier. This ensures that the supplier will issue an appropriate credit invoice.

Each day all invoices for goods delivered that day will be listed on a daily food receiving report. This report, when totaled, indicates the value of goods that have gone into direct purchases (and are assumed to have gone immediately into production) and

# DAILY RECORD OF PURCHASES AND ISSUES

HOTEL _____

DEPT. _____ DATE _____ 19 ____ DAY OF WEEK _____

| PURCHASES | | | STOCK TO STOREROOM | | | | | BAR | | | |
|---|---|---|---|---|---|---|---|---|---|---|---|
| 1 | 2 | 3 | 4 | 5 | 6 | 7 | 8 | 9 | 10 | 11 | 12 |
| NAME OF FIRM | AMOUNT OF INVOICE | DIRECT ISSUES TO KITCHEN | MEAT, FISH & POULTRY | STAPLES | FRUITS & VEGETABLES | DIARY PRODUCTS | LIQUOR | BEER | WINE | MIXES INGRED. | CARTAGE |
| | | | | | | | | | | | |
| A | TODAY'S PURCHASES | | | | | | | | | | |
| B | BALANCE FORWARD from Yesterday | | | | | | | | | | |
| C | TOTAL TO DATE THIS MONTH | | | | | | | | | | |

| 13 | 14 | 15 | 16 | 17 | 18 | 19 | 20 | 21 | 22 | 23 | 24 | 25 |
|---|---|---|---|---|---|---|---|---|---|---|---|---|
| | | | | DIRECT ISSUES | | | | | | | | FOOD COST 14 to 24 |
| | MEAT | FISH | POULTRY | FRUITS | VEGET | DAIRY PRODUCTS | BAKERY PRODUCTS | STAPLES | COFFEE | BUTTER | EGG'S | |
| | | | | | | | | | | | | |
| D | DIRECT ISS. | | | | | | | | | | | |
| E | STORES ISS. | | | | | | | | | | | |
| F | TOTAL ISS. | | | | | | | | | | | |
| G | FWD. BAL. | | | | | | | | | | | |
| H | TOTAL M/D | | | | | | | | | | | |

| I | BEGINNING INVENTORY LAST MONTH END | | |
|---|---|---|---|
| J | STOCK TO STORE ROOM C4 to 7 | 5c | |
| K | STORE ROOM ISSUES E14 to 24 | 21 to 25 | |
| L | (I + J - K) BALANCE ON HAND | | |
| M | PHYSICAL INVENTORY | | |
| N | (L + OR - M) ADJUSTMENT $ | | |
| O | (N% to M) ADJUSTMENT % | | |
| P | (SALES/M) INVENTORY TURNOVER | | |

**Figure 4.6** A more comprehensive type of daily food (and in this case beverage) receiving report used in larger hotels.

those that have gone into the storeroom. This information is necessary in order to calculate a food cost percentage on a daily and an accumulated basis, and to aid in storeroom control.

## DISCUSSION QUESTIONS

1. List some of the major standard practices in receiving food.

2. What is a credit memorandum and why should it be signed by the delivery driver?

3. Generally, what is the difference between the type of food that is put into the storeroom and food that is considered to be direct purchases?

4. Why is a breakdown of purchases into various categories (such as meat, poultry, fish) of value?

5. Describe how the daily food receiving report is used.

## MULTIPLE CHOICE/DISCUSSION QUESTIONS

1. The daily food receiving report
   a. Lists in detail, item by item, all food purchases made each day.
   b. Summarizes daily food purchases from invoices.
   c. Is used to tell the receiver what items have been ordered and will be received that day.
   d. Breaks down purchases into categories so that a daily food cost can be calculated.
   e. Serves a purpose other than any of the above.

2. Direct purchases are called that because
   a. They are put directly into the storeroom when delivered.
   b. They are shipped directly from the supplier when ordered.
   c. They go directly from the storeroom into food production areas.
   d. They are put straight into production when received and are considered to be used up that day.
   e. The receiver has been directed by management to put them into storeroom or refrigerator areas.

3. An analysis of purchases by category is useful for indicating
   a. Which supplier is getting the largest share of the purchase dollar.
   b. Which categories are being purchased more frequently than others.
   c. That the ordering/purchasing and receiving control procedures are working effectively.
   d. That prices of certain items are rising faster than others.
   e. That a change in the breakdown of the purchase dollar has occurred which may be the cause of a change in the food cost.

## PROBLEMS

1. The following invoices are on hand for food purchases made on June 10.

| Company | Item | Total Amount | Distribution |
|---------|------|--------------|--------------|
| Prairie Meats | Fresh meat | $84.32 | In kitchen refrigerators |
| Hubbard Bakery | Bakery goods | 15.15 | To dining room |
| Coast Fishing Co. | Fish | 21.94 | Fresh, $6.51; balance canned items to storeroom |
| Macdonalds | Canned fruit and vegetables | 71.45 | To storeroom |
| T. Lee Co. | Fresh fruit and vegetables | 25.14 | In kitchen refrigerators |
| Valley Dairy | Dairy goods | 18.40 | In kitchen refrigerators except $4.34 for cream and eggs for cocktail lounge |
| Miller Flour Co. | Bulk flour | 41.18 | To storeroom |

Complete the daily food receiving report from the above information.

2. The following invoices are on hand for food items received on August 31.

| Company | Items | Amount | Distribution |
|---------|-------|--------|--------------|
| Seaboard | Fish | $51.51 | $21.63 was for fresh items, balance canned fish delivered to the store-room. |
| Mission Canners | Fruit and vegetables | 65.91 | All for stores |
| J. V. Smith | Fresh produce | 31.27 | $2.86 for limes for the cocktail lounge, balance direct purchases. |
| Country Produce | Dairy produce | 17.15 | $1.20 for eggs for cocktail lounge, balance direct purchases. |

| Company | Items | Amount | Distribution |
|---------|-------|--------|--------------|
| Liquid Bottlers | Soft drinks | 37.23 | $2.08 for bottles (returnable), balance for contents put into stores. |
| Meat Packers | Meat | 196.56 | Put into kitchen refrigerators |
| Allgood | Flour | 25.75 | All for stores |
| Central Bakery | Bread | 15.09 | All for kitchen |
| Robinson | Poultry | 18.53 | All for kitchen |
| Creamland | Dairy produce | 15.27 | All for kitchen |
| Coast Suppliers (credit memorandum) | Canned items | (13.18) | Canned peaches (wrong size) returned to supplier. Originally billed on Aug. 28, and appeared on receiving report of that date; storeroom item |
| Seaboard Fish (credit memorandum) | Fresh fish | (9.87) | Fish included on invoice above $51.51, but not of acceptable quality |

Prepare the daily food receiving report for August 31.

3. The Fine Food drive-in restaurant had the following breakdown of purchases for the first ten days in September, as shown in Table 4.2. Previous experience and information indicates that the breakdown of the purchase dollar by category has been

| Item | Percent |
|------|---------|
| Meat | 17.0 % |
| Fish | 6.0 |
| Poultry | 6.0 |
| Produce | 10.0 |
| Groceries | 19.0 |
| Frozen food | 3.0 |
| Bread, pastry | 12.0 |
| Milk, cream | 15.0 |
| Butter, eggs | 10.0 |
| Ice cream | 1.0 |
| Fountain supplies | 1.0 |
| | 100.0 % |

a. For the ten-day period, add up, by category, the total dollar cost.
b. Add up the Total column.
c. Express each category total as a percent of the Total column addition.
d. Comment on the results obtained.

**Table 4.2**

| Day | Meat | Fish | Poultry | Produce | Grocery | Frozen Food | Bread, Pastry | Milk, Cream | Butter, Eggs | Ice Cream | Fountain Supply | Total |
|---|---|---|---|---|---|---|---|---|---|---|---|---|
| 1 | $83.84 | $25.25 | $47.75 | $40.87 | $148.05 | — | $50.68 | $65.24 | $30.60 | — | — | $492.28 |
| 2 | — | — | — | 60.99 | 128.55 | — | 71.74 | 79.24 | — | $4.50 | — | 345.02 |
| 3 | — | — | — | 41.00 | 78.12 | $13.56 | 26.56 | 86.56 | 91.50 | — | — | 337.30 |
| 4 | 124.54 | 49.50 | — | 35.01 | 43.90 | 9.30 | 60.76 | 73.62 | — | — | — | 396.63 |
| 5 | 95.10 | 10.80 | 76.21 | 37.80 | 132.70 | — | 45.47 | 54.16 | 34.50 | 3.70 | $10.70 | 501.14 |
| 6 | 99.45 | 47.85 | — | 42.23 | 70.32 | — | 63.00 | 97.54 | 30.60 | 7.40 | — | 458.39 |
| 7 | 134.71 | 20.75 | 131.31 | 54.27 | 105.76 | — | 69.01 | 80.70 | 60.90 | (.80) credit | — | 656.61 |
| 8 | 56.64 | — | — | 50.18 | 35.16 | 61.00 | 34.16 | 84.33 | 65.10 | 3.70 | — | 390.27 |
| 9 | 133.30 | 49.50 | — | 58.62 | 4.20 | — | 68.88 | 79.92 | — | — | — | 394.42 |
| 10 | 175.92 | — | 71.89 | 27.68 | — | 22.68 | 48.56 | 69.29 | 34.50 | — | — | 450.52 |

# 5

# Food Stores and Inventory Control

## Objectives

After studying this chapter, the reader will be able to

1. List four features about storeroom design or location.
2. Describe (or draw an outline of) a perpetual inventory card, a bin card, and a requisition.
3. Give a one-sentence description of the purpose of a perpetual inventory card, a bin card, and a requisition, and state how and by whom each form is completed.
4. Use the "most recent price" method of recording prices on perpetual inventory cards.
5. Describe in two or three sentences the procedure for taking inventory in a food storeroom and the use of inventory sheets, or inventory books.
6. Define "open stock" inventory (as opposed to "storeroom" inventory) and, given appropriate information, calculate the dollar amount of "open stock" at month-end.
7. Calculate a food inventory turnover.
8. Complete a perpetual inventory card from invoice and requisition information and list the steps to take to try and reconcile a difference at month-end between the perpetual inventory card figure and the actual count of items in the storeroom.

All perishable food, on receipt, is distributed into coolers and refrigerators or into other storage areas close to the production areas (kitchens). These direct purchases are put straight into production and are assumed to be used up within the next twenty-four hours. The fact that this is not always the case creates some difficulties (as we shall see later) if we want to calculate our food cost percentage on a daily basis. Staples, canned goods, and similar products that have a fairly long shelf life are put into a separate locked storeroom.

## THE STOREROOM

### Location and Design

There should be only one main storeroom for food items, located on the same level as the delivery entrance and, if possible, on the same level as the main kitchen and close to it. Such a location will reduce movement and handling of goods to a minimum and thus reduce "leakage" of food items. The storeroom should be designed so that food is stored in sectionalized compartments which can be easily labeled. No food should be stored directly on the floor. High turnover items should be placed in readily accessible places, preferably close to the storeroom door or counter. Heavy items (such as 100 lb sacks of flour) should be similarly located.

Once items are placed in particular areas or shelves and the shelves have been labeled, item locations should be changed as infrequently as possible. Familiarity with the location of items means time-saving efficiency when storing and issuing them. Furthermore, stock-taking is facilitated. Inventory sheets can be preprinted with all items carried in stock, and the listing of the items on these stock sheets can coincide with the order in which the items are located on the shelves.

### Control

There are two main reasons for control of items in the storeroom: (1) To prevent loss (and thus control costs) of items stored therein; (2) to charge the various departments that receive food items from the storeroom with the cost of these items. To have complete control of what comes in and goes out of the storeroom, two forms are required: (1) Perpetual inventory cards and (2) requisitions.

## CONTROL FORMS

### Perpetual Inventory Cards

A perpetual inventory card is illustrated in Figure 5.2. One card is required for each type and size of item carried in stock. The figures in the In column are taken from the invoices for goods delivered to stores. If the receiver is also the storekeeper, he or she can complete this task at the end of the day after finishing the daily food receiving report. Otherwise the receiver must pass the invoices to the storekeeper. Figures in the Out column are entered from requisitions given to the storekeeper from various persons authorized to request food items from stores (requisitions will be discussed in a later section). It is obvious that if all figures are correctly entered and no unauthorized goods are taken from the storeroom, the Balance column will indicate exactly how many of each item there should be on hand in the storeroom at any time.

**Figure 5.1** Comprehensive control of the food storeroom can be obtained by using perpetual inventory cards and requisitions.

| PERPETUAL INVENTORY CARD | | | | | | | |
|---|---|---|---|---|---|---|---|
| Item _Tomato Juice – Gallons_ | | | Cost _0.87¢_ Cost _0.90¢_ | | | | |
| Date | In | Out | Balance | Date | In | Out | Balance |
| | | | *fwd.* 6 | | | | |
| *Oct. 1* | 12 | 2 | 16 | | | | |
| 2 | | 4 | 12 | | | | |
| 4 | | 1 | 11 | | | | |
| 7 | | 6 | 5 | | | | |
| | | | | | | | |
| Suppliers | | Tel. #s | | Maximum __24 (4 cases)__ | | | |
| *Macdonald* | | *681-4322* | | Minimum __6 (1 case)__ | | | |
| *Western Supply* | | *542-7165* | | | | | |
| *Hardy & Co.* | | *921-3012* | | | | | |

**Figure 5.2** The perpetual inventory card is completed from invoices (In) and requisitions (Out) and gives a running (perpetual) Balance of the quantity of each item kept in stores.

Perpetual inventory cards can generally be completed by the storekeeper. A dishonest storekeeper could, of course, take items from the storeroom for his personal use and adjust the Balance column of the card to hide this theft. The control over this is to have the accounting office spot-check a certain number of cards each month, tracing quantities on the cards back to the related invoice or requisition to ensure that the entries are correct, and checking the arithmetic to ensure that the Balance figure is correct. Alternatively, the cards could be maintained by someone in the control office who has no access to the storeroom and would not therefore be tempted to "cook" the balances. If the storekeeper does not keep the perpetual inventory cards, then he or she should be provided with bin cards.

As well as serving a control function, perpetual inventory cards can have a number of other purposes:

1. They aid in inventory count at month-end.
2. They carry the prices of goods received and thus are invaluable in costing out requisitions.
3. They can carry the names, addresses, and telephone numbers of suppliers.
4. For each individual item, they can show what the maximum quantity should be and what the minimum quantity (reorder level) is.

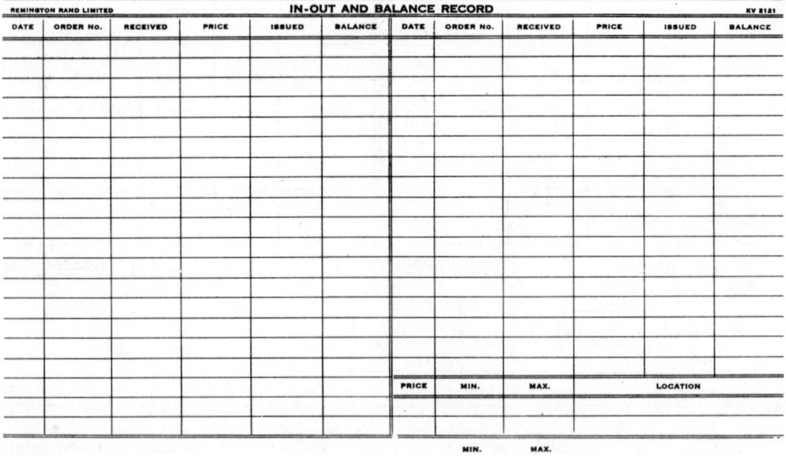
ITEM

REMINGTON RAND LIMITED IN-OUT AND BALANCE RECORD KV 2121

| DATE | ORDER No. | RECEIVED | PRICE | ISSUED | BALANCE | DATE | ORDER No. | RECEIVED | PRICE | ISSUED | BALANCE |
|---|---|---|---|---|---|---|---|---|---|---|---|

PRICE MIN. MAX. LOCATION

MIN. MAX.

**Figure 5.3** A type of perpetual inventory card that could be used for control of food storeroom items.

5. They can indicate, at a glance, which items are slow-moving and are tying up money (the chef could then be notified to feature a menu item that would use up this "dead" stock).

## Pricing on Cards

Although there are a number of methods of pricing items on perpetual inventory cards, for simplicity's sake it is recommended that the most recent price be used. In other words, if there are ten items on hand at $1 each, and twenty-four more are received at $1.10 each, from that point on all thirty-four items on hand will be considered to be valued at $1.10. It is true that, arithmetically, this is not the most accurate method, but for all practical purposes it will give results that are accurate enough, will cut down on calculations otherwise required, will speed up the pricing of requisitions, and will not lead to any loss of control. Finally, again for simplicity, prices need not be carried in fractions of cents.

## Bin Cards

Bin cards (see Figure 5.4) are similar to perpetual inventory cards; they have columns that allow the storekeeper to enter deliveries and issues for each separate item in stock, and at any time the Balance column indicates what is still on hand and what

| BIN CARD | | | |
|---|---|---|---|
| ITEM _Tomato Juice - gall_ | | | |
| Date | In | Out | Balance |
| | | | fwd. 6 |
| Oct. 1 | 12 | 2 | 16 |
| 2 | | 4 | 12 |
| 4 | | 1 | 11 |
| 7 | | 6 | 5 |
| | | | |
| | | | |
| | | | |
| | | | |

**Figure 5.4** The bin card is a simplified version of the perpetual inventory card.

must be reordered. But bin cards do not serve any *control* function. They are simply for storekeeping information.

### Requisitions

The other form required for complete storeroom control is the requisition. A sample requisition is illustrated in Figure 5.5. A requisition is simply a request from a department (dining room, coffee shop, lounge, kitchen) for food supplies from the storeroom. The following procedures should be used for controlling requisitions:

1. Blank pads of requisitions, in duplicate, should be made available only to those authorized to complete and sign them.
2. The original, listing requirements and quantities, is delivered to the storekeeper. The duplicate is kept in the department so that what is delivered from stores can be checked.
3. The storekeeper should be supplied with a list of the signatures of those who have authority to sign requisitions.
4. The storekeeper should not have access to any blank requisitions.

In addition, requisitions can be numbered and printed on different colors of paper for quick identification of the initiating department. In many small establishments it would also be wise, if the storekeeper has a number of other jobs to do, to limit the hours during which goods can be issued from stores.

### Completion of Requisitions

When the storekeeper has finished issuing the goods he fills in the Quantity Supplied column (which may or may not agree with the Quantity Ordered column depending on whether or not there was enough of that item in stores). He then enters the Quantity Supplied figure in the Out column of his perpetual inventory card, and from the card copies the item cost price onto the Unit Cost column of the requisition. Requisitions can subsequently be extended and totaled.

### Dispensing with Perpetual Inventory Cards and/or Requisitions

Since not all food items can be controlled under a storeroom situation, many people believe it is a waste of time and money to have perpetual inventory cards and requisitions for only

| Items | Quantity Ordered | Quantity Supplied | Unit Cost | Total |
|---|---|---|---|---|
| REQUISITION | | Date *Oct. 1* | | |
| Tomato Juice - gall | 2 | 2 | 0.90 | 1.80 |
| Orange Juice - gall | 1 | 1 | 1.14 | 1.14 |
| Asparagus - 10 oz | 4 | 4 | 0.42 | 1.68 |
| Beets - 24 oz. | 1 | 1 | 0.35 | 0.35 |
| Sugar - 100 lb. | 1 | 1 | 20.30 | 20.30 |
| TOTAL | | | | 25.27 |

Authorized signature _D. Sinclair_

**Figure 5.5** The Item and Quantity Ordered columns of the requisition are filled in by the person requiring the goods. The Quantity Supplied, Unit Cost, and Total columns are subsequently completed by the storekeeper.

Nº 08031

FOOD STOREROOM REQUISITION

DEPARTMENT _____     DATE _____

| QUAN-TITY | ARTICLE AND DESCRIPTION | NUMBER WEIGHT | UNIT PRICE | AMOUNT | |
|---|---|---|---|---|---|
| | | | | | |
| | | | | | |
| | | | | | |
| | | | | | |
| | | | | | |
| | | | | | |
| | | | | | |
| | | | | | |
| | | | | | |
| | | | | | |
| | | | | | |
| | | | | | |
| | | | | | |
| | | | | | |
| | | | | | |
| | | | | | |
| | | | | | |

ORDERED BY _____     FILLED BY _____

AUTHORIZED BY _____     RECEIVED BY _____

**Figure 5.6** A typical storeroom requisition.

this part of the food inventory. However, even if only 25 percent of total food deliveries go into the storeroom and are controlled, there is that much less to worry about in terms of loss.

Many small establishments do not have the time or the staff to operate a complete system of food stores control but still wish to know the cost of issues from the storeroom each day so that they can subsequently calculate a daily food cost percentage (see Chapter 6). If perpetual inventory cards are dispensed with to reduce paperwork, one method of keeping track of the cost of items in the storeroom is to write or stamp the cost onto the package, can, container, or case. This should be done when the goods are received and the invoice is readily available. Without some record of the cost of items, it is difficult to calculate an inventory value on inventory sheets at month-end; it is also difficult to cost out requisitions.

In smaller establishments where there is no storekeeper and the storeroom is, of necessity, accessible to a number of people who require food supplies, there would not be any real need for requisitions. If information concerning the daily total value of food taken from stores and put into production is still required for food-costing purposes, all that is needed is a sheet of paper on which the headings shown in Figure 5.7 are entered.

Those who remove items from stores should be instructed to record on this sheet all items, quantities, and costs as goods are taken. The sheet could be clipped to the door of the storeroom or located in an equally obvious spot so that the staff is constantly reminded to fill in the details required. At the end of each day the sheet can be removed and replaced with a fresh one. The information it contains can be used to multiply quantities by costs and then the total can be added. This information, we will see in

| Date _____ | | |
|-------------------------------|----------|-----------|
| Item | Quantity | Unit Cost |
| | | |
| | | |

Figure 5.7

Chapter 6, will be useful for calculating a daily food cost percentage.

## INVENTORY

### Procedure

Food storeroom inventory is usually taken once a month, at month-end. Two people from the control office should take stock. One person counts the quantity of each item, and the second person verifies that the figure agrees with the perpetual inventory card Balance. At the same time, this quantity can be recorded on the inventory sheet (see below). If the count and the card Balance figures do not agree, a recount should be made. The difference could be the result of some items having inadvertently been put in some other part of the storeroom. If the two figures still do not agree, then the card Balance figure must be changed to reflect the *actual* count (needless to say, the *actual* count is also the one that will be recorded on the inventory sheet).

**Figure 5.8** Complete and periodic inventory-taking is an integral part of a good food control system.

Differences can also sometimes be caused by deliveries received on the last day of the month having been put into the storeroom without the invoice information having yet been posted to the perpetual inventory card. Similarly, requisitions may have been completed just prior to stock-taking without the information yet having been used to adjust card figures downward. These possibilities should be checked to reconcile differences between card balance and inventory count. In order to make stock-taking easier, perpetual inventory cards should be in the same order as the items on the shelves, and in the same order as the inventory sheet listing.

### Inventory Sheets

Inventory sheets are usually columnar in arrangement, with columns headed Item, Quantity, Unit Cost, Total. These sheets should be preprinted and should list all items carried in stock, in the order in which the items appear on the shelves. As the items are counted and compared with the perpetual inventory cards, the quantity can be recorded on the inventory sheet. At the same time, the cost of the item can be copied from the card on to the inventory sheet. After stock-taking, the inventory sheets are individually extended and totaled. The accumulated total of all sheets is, obviously, the total value of food in the storeroom.

### Inventory Book

Instead of using individual inventory sheets, an inventory book can be kept. The items on hand, as can be seen by the illustration in Figure 5.9, are written only once on the left-hand side. Columns with the same headings as those on an inventory sheet then permit the recording of Quantity, Unit Cost, and Total for a number of successive months. Such a book has advantages. For example, price changes and slow-moving items can be detected more quickly. The main disadvantage of such a stock book is that if any major relocation of items occurs in the storeroom, the book is not as flexible as inventory sheets.

| INVENTORY BOOK | | October | | | November | | | |
|---|---|---|---|---|---|---|---|---|
| | | Quantity | Unit Cost | Total | Quantity | Unit Cost | Total | Qua |
| Balance forward | | | | 2082.01 | | | | |
| Juice – Apple | 46 oz. | 11 | 0.30 | 3.30 | | | | |
| Carrot | 12 oz. | 24 | 0.09 | 2.16 | | | | |
| Pineapple | 46 oz. | 6 | 0.36 | 2.16 | | | | |
| Grape | 46 oz. | 8 | 0.40 | 3.20 | | | | |
| V-8 | 46 oz. | 12 | 0.37 | 4.44 | | | | |
| | | | | | | | | |
| | | | | | | | | |
| | | | | 2097.27 | | | | |

**Figure 5.9** The inventory book, for recording the value of all items on hand at each month-end in the storeroom.

## Open Stock Inventory

The storeroom, however, is not the only area where there is an inventory of food. At any time, there has to be a certain carryover of food in the kitchens and other production areas in readiness for the following day's business. To determine the value of this stock at each month-end is quite difficult. In addition to items purchased in their "raw" state, there may be soups, stocks, sauces, and combination dishes in a state of preparation that are not easy to cost out. But some value must be attached to these items so that a fairly accurate estimate can be made for inventory purposes. In some cases an estimate may be made only once, at the end of the first month, and increased or decreased at the end of each subsequent month based on the chef's best guess as to how much more or less open stock there is in dollar terms. One useful method for calculating this increase or decrease is to pick a major item or items and use the change in their value to reflect the change in all items.

For example, let us assume that the previous month-end inventory of open stock was $2,000. Included in this is 500 lb of meat at an average cost of $1 per pound, or $500 (this $500 represents a fair portion – 25 percent – of the total open stock inventory). The following month-end there are 550 lb at $1.10 per pound, a total of $605. Since the meat part of the inventory has gone up by $105, or 21 percent (105/500 x 100), then it would seem reasonable to assume that total inventory has increased by 21 percent. In this case, our new month-end open stock inventory would be estimated to be valued at

$$\$2,000 + (21\% \times \$2,000) \text{ or } \$2,000 + \$420 = \$2,420$$

There may also be month-ends when this open stock has to be further increased. If a heavy purchase was necessary on the last day or two of the month because of a long weekend or because an unusually large function was to take place early the following month, the amount of this heavy purchase should be added to the normal level of open stock value. Alternatively, if stock-taking occurred at the end of a long weekend, the amount of open stock on hand could be unusually low, and its value should be reduced accordingly.

### Inventory Turnover

How much food inventory (both storeroom and open stock) should a typical establishment have? For each individual item, maximum quantity limits and minimum (reorder point) quantity levels can be established and the information recorded on the relevant perpetual inventory card (see Figure 5.2). But in addition to quantity, the total dollar value invested should also be considered. Too much money tied up in inventory means that the excess investment is not earning income it otherwise could (for example, interest in a bank account is being lost). Similarly, too little invested could indicate that not enough is being carried to handle peak volume, and customers are being lost.

One useful business ratio, known as *inventory turnover*, can be used to calculate the right amount. In the restaurant business, the average turnover rate appears to be between two to four times a month. Although there are exceptions to the guidelines, most operators who receive delivery of food items on a daily basis find that their inventory turnover is within these limits. This turnover rate is calculated as follows:

$$\frac{\text{Food cost for the month}}{\text{Average inventory}}$$

Food cost (discussed in more detail in the next chapter) can be calculated using the following general formula:

Beginning of the month inventory    *6,000*

\+

Purchases during month    *+20,500*

−

End of the month inventory    *− 7,000*

=

Food cost for the month    *= 19,500*

Average inventory is calculated as follows:

Beginning of the month inventory    *6,000*

\+

End of the month inventory    *+ 7,000*

÷

2    *÷13,000 ÷2 = 6,500*

    *19,500 (3)*

Assuming the following:

| | |
|---|---|
| Beginning of the month inventory | $6,000 |
| End of month inventory | 7,000 |
| Purchases during month | 20,500 |

our inventory turnover would be

$$\frac{\$6,000 + \$20,500 - \$7,000}{(\$6,000 + \$7,000) \div 2} = \frac{\$19,500}{\$6,500} = 3 \text{ times}$$

## SUMMARY

Food storeroom control can be achieved with the use of two forms: the perpetual inventory card and the requisition. Perpetual inventory cards, one for each item in the storeroom, are completed from invoices and requisitions. The invoice quantities are recorded in the In column, and the requisition quantities in the Out column. Requisitions are made out and signed by authorized personnel requesting food items from the storeroom. If the perpetual inventory cards are completed correctly, they will give, at any point in time, in the Balance column, the amount (quantity) of each item that should be in the storeroom.

These cards can also serve other functions. For example, they should carry the cost of each item, using the cost taken from the invoice of the most recent purchase (information needed for costing out requisitions); they can show the names, addresses, and telephone numbers of suppliers of that item; they can indicate the maximum and minimum quantities of that item that should be carried; and they can indicate slow-moving stock. A simplified version of the perpetual inventory card is known as a bin card.

When inventory is taken at month-end, the quantities on the cards should agree with the count of items on the shelves. Differences should be reconciled by checking through the related invoices and requisitions of that item since the last stock-taking. If the cause of the differences cannot be discovered, the Balance figure on the card must always be adjusted to reflect the *actual* count.

The value of inventory in the storeroom can be calculated using inventory sheets, or an inventory book. To this value must be added the value of the open stock (inventory in refrigerators, in production in the kitchen, or in other related areas). It is also helpful to calculate how quickly inventory is used. This is usually done in terms of a ratio called inventory turnover. The general equation for calculating this is $\dfrac{\text{Food cost for the month.}}{\text{Average inventory}}$ In the food industry, this turnover figure generally ranges between two and four times a month.

## DISCUSSION QUESTIONS

1. What are some of the main points to remember about storeroom location and design?

2. Describe, or illustrate, a perpetual inventory card. Explain how it is used and the purposes it serves.

3. What is the difference between a perpetual inventory card and a bin card?

4. The easiest method of pricing items kept in the food storeroom is the "most recent" one. How does this method work?

5. What are requisitions, and who initiates them?

6. Which columns on the requisition does the storekeeper complete, and where does he get the information?

7. Describe the procedure for taking inventory in the food storeroom.

8. What is open stock food inventory?

9. What is the equation for inventory turnover?

## MULTIPLE CHOICE/DISCUSSION QUESTIONS

1. Perpetual inventory cards for food storeroom items
   a. Control perishables, such as fresh fruit and vegetables.
   b. Eliminate the need to take inventory at month-end.
   c. Aid in the control of items recorded on the cards.
   d. Guarantee that unauthorized staff remove nothing from the storeroom.
   e. Serve a purpose, or purposes, other than any of the above.

2. Requisitions are used
   a. To allow staff to help themselves to storeroom items.
   b. To give, by adding them up, the total cost of food put into direct production each day.
   c. To order food from the storeroom for delivery to the various departments in a hotel or restaurant.
   d. To calculate month-end inventory turnover.
   e. For none of the above purposes.

3. A food inventory turnover of four in a typical restaurant would mean that inventory is turned over (or used up) on average
   a. Once every four weeks.
   b. Once every four months.
   c. Four times a year.
   d. Four times a month.
   e. Four times a week.
   f. None of the above.

## PROBLEMS

1. The Ritz Restaurant has a food cost for the month of $31,200. At the beginning of the month its food inventory was $9,750; at the end of the month, $10,250. What was its inventory turnover rate for the month?

2. A cafeteria in a downtown location that has daily delivery of purchases has an average monthly food cost of $20,000. In dollars, between what upper and lower limits might its food inventory be expected to be?

3. The open stock inventory of the Classy Cafe was estimated to be $800 on October 1. Included were meat and poultry items which, when costed out, were valued at $260. On October 31 the open stock value of meat and poultry items was costed out at $286. What would be the estimated total value of open stock inventory at month-end?

4. You have the following information: November 1 total food inventory, $3,150; food purchases during November, $9,450; November 30 total food inventory, $2,740. Calculate the inventory turnover rate for November to the nearest one decimal place.

5. In a hotel's food storeroom on October 31 the perpetual inventory card for a certain item of canned fruit showed there were 25 cans on hand at a cost of $0.74 per can. A physical count of the items on the shelf confirmed that the quantity was correct.

Information extracted from invoices in November indicated that the following purchases of this item were made:

November  9: 2 cases (6 cans per case) @ $4.56 per case
November 13: 2 cases (6 cans per case) @ $4.62 per case
November 19: 4 cases (6 cans per case) @ $4.74 per case
November 22: 4 cases (6 cans per case) @ $4.56 per case

Information taken from requisitions processed during the month showed that the following quantities of this canned fruit were issued:

November  2: 12 cans
November  4:  3 cans
November  8:  5 cans
November 12: 12 cans
November 15:  6 cans
November 20: 18 cans
November 21:  2 cans

November 24:  3 cans
November 28:  6 cans
November 30:  3 cans

a. Prepare a blank perpetual inventory card and complete the In and Out columns from the information extracted from invoices and requisitions, respectively.

b. Record on the card unit (can) cost changes as they occur and the date each change occurs. Calculate these unit costs to the nearest whole cent, using the "most recent" cost price method.

c. For each date on which there was a requisition, show the unit cost that would appear on that requisition.

d. Calculate the total value that would appear on the inventory sheet for this item on November 30.

6. At month-end the actual count of a certain item in the food storeroom was less than the Balance figure on the related perpetual inventory card. List, in logical order, the steps you could take to try to discover the cause of this difference.

# 6

# Receiving Report Summary

## Objectives

After studying this chapter, the reader will be able to

1. List the three steps the accounting office must take to audit a completed daily food receiving report.
2. Give the two purposes of a receiving report summary.
3. Identify the source of information for each of the columns on a receiving report summary.
4. Identify and describe how each of the two month-end adjustments are carried out on a receiving report summary.
5. Describe how meat tags can aid in food cost control.
6. Complete and balance from given data a receiving report summary on a daily or a monthly basis.

At the end of each day the receiver and/or storekeeper forward to the control office the following:

1. The daily food receiving report
2. The invoices for food purchases for that day
3. The requisitions for items issued from the food storeroom that day.

The control office should then check:

1. That invoices have been properly extended and totaled by the supplier (prices should also be checked from time to time against the market quotation sheet).
2. That invoices have been correctly listed on the daily food receiving report and that the columns of that report have been correctly added.
3. That requisitions have been correctly extended and totaled (requisition cost figures should also be checked from time to time against the perpetual inventory card cost figures).

Once this work has been completed, the control office can

complete the receiving report summary (see Figure 6.1), a form that serves two purposes: (1) It is an aid in storeroom inventory control; and (2) it permits a calculation of a daily food cost percentage and an accumulated (to date) food cost percentage.

## HOW THE SUMMARY IS COMPLETED

The Opening Inventory figure on the first day of the month is the *actual inventory value* of food in the storeroom from the previous month-end stock-taking. The Storeroom Purchases column is completed by transferring each day's Storeroom column total of the daily food receiving report. The Storeroom Issues column is the total of all requisitions for issues from food stores for that day. The Closing Inventory figure each day is brought forward and becomes the Opening Inventory amount for the next day.

The Closing Inventory column requires a calculation:

Opening inventory

+

Storeroom purchases

−

Storeroom issues

=

Closing inventory

In this way, each day during the month, a running balance can be kept of the value of food stored in the storeroom. At the month-end, the final day's Closing Inventory can be compared with that month-end actual (physical) inventory. The two figures will probably not agree because of errors in issuing items without a requisition, in pricing requisitions, in failing to record deliveries that had no accompanying invoices on the daily food receiving report, and so on. However, the two figures should be relatively close, and any difference will be used as an adjustment in calculating the month-end food cost percentage (this will be explained later). In any event, the *actual food inventory* figure at month-end is the one that is put into the Opening Inventory column on day 1 of the following month's receiving report summary.

RECEIVING REPORT SUMMARY                    Month of ___November___

| Date | Opening Inventory | Storeroom Purchases | Storeroom Issues | Closing Inventory | Direct Purchases | Transfers In | Transfers Out | Employee Meals | Net Food Cost Today | Net Food Cost To-date | Sales Today | Sales To-date | Food Cost % Today | Food Cost % To-date |
|---|---|---|---|---|---|---|---|---|---|---|---|---|---|---|
| 1 | 2103.04 | 142.10 | 71.80 | 2173.34 | 331.09 | 17.06 | 4.72 | 31.50 | 383.73 | | 1110.15 | | 34.6 | |
| 2 | 2173.34 | 107.20 | 108.03 | 2172.51 | 274.72 | | 16.04 | 29.50 | 337.21 | 720.94 | 1251.70 | 2361.85 | 26.9 | 30.5 |
| 3 | 2172.51 | | 24.11 | 2148.40 | | | | 15.00 | 9.11 | 730.05 | 742.10 | 3103.95 | 1.2 | 23.5 |
| 4 | 2148.40 | 43.80 | 161.92 | 2030.28 | 421.18 | 8.40 | 3.22 | 32.00 | 556.28 | 1286.33 | 1171.90 | 4275.85 | 47.5 | 30.1 |
| 5 | 2030.28 | 191.06 | 79.16 | 2142.18 | 377.25 | | 1.17 | 34.50 | 420.74 | 1707.07 | 1320.55 | 5596.40 | 31.9 | 30.5 |
| 6 | 2142.18 | 72.14 | 92.08 | 2122.24 | 211.94 | | 1.10 | 29.00 | 260.92 | 1967.99 | 1206.95 | 6803.35 | 21.6 | 28.9 |
| 7 | 2122.24 | 83.90 | 43.10 | 2163.04 | | | | | | | | | | |
| | | | | | 200.14 | 14.10 | | 27.50 | 174.15 | 8767.69 | 817.20 | 28525.15 | 21.8 | 30.4 |
| | | | | | | | | 32.00 | 243.18 | 9010.87 | 1118.40 | 29644.15 | 21.8 | 30.0 |
| 29 | 2040.21 | 173.04 | 47.99 | 2165.26 | 178.40 | 9.20 | | 31.00 | 204.59 | 9215.46 | 1041.80 | 30685.95 | 19.6 | 30.0 |
| 30 | 2165.26 | 61.02 | 102.10 | 2124.18 | 317.22 | | 9.30 | 34.50 | 375.52 | 9590.98 | 1211.35 | 31897.30 | 31.0 | 30.1 |
| 31 | | | | | | | | | | | | | | |

Actual Inventory .......... 2097.27

Difference ................ 26.91

Adjustments to Food Cost  –  Storeroom Inventory Difference    + 26.91

                             –  Open Stock Change                 – 420.00

ADJUSTED MONTH-END FOOD COST ................. 9197.89

MONTH END FOOD COST PERCENTAGE   $\dfrac{9197.89}{31{,}897.30} \times 100 = 28.84\%$

**Figure 6.1** The receiving report summary is useful for summarizing the figures from each day's daily food receiving reports; it aids in food storeroom inventory control and permits calculation of food cost percentages on a daily and accumulated (to date) basis.

## Calculation of Daily and Accumulated Food Cost Percentage

The rest of the columns on the receiving report summary are used in calculating the daily and accumulated (to date) food cost percentage. The Direct Purchases column is completed by transferring the total of the Direct Purchases column from each day's daily food receiving report. The Transfers In column is the total of any requisitions for interdepartmental transfers of food or related items. For example, the kitchen could have requisitioned some wine for cooking from the bar. Even though the requisition does not affect the food storeroom, it is still an addition to the food department's cost of production, and would be entered in this column.

The Transfers Out column would be the total of any requisitions of the following two types: (1) Transfers of goods from the kitchen (or other production area of the food department) to some other department. An example would be cream or eggs transferred from kitchen refrigerators to the cocktail lounge. (2) Items included in the Storeroom Issues figure which, although reducing the value of food in the storeroom, should not be charged as a cost to the food department. An example could be cans of olives or cherries requisitioned from food stores by the cocktail lounge.

The cost of employee meals for the day should be entered in the Employee Meals column. Even if all employees pay for their meals in a staff cafeteria, these sales and costs should be kept separate from sales and costs of meals served to guests because generally the two types of meals have different markups; if we mixed up the two, we would have a distorted figure of food cost for meals served to guests. If there is no employee cafeteria or no meal check of any kind in use, which is often the case where employees have free meals, then this cost will have to be estimated. This is not too difficult to do from payroll records: count the number of employees on duty each day and multiply that figure by a predetermined estimated cost per employee meal consumed.

## INTER-KITCHEN  TRANSFER

### N° 24401

FROM _____

TO _____

FOR _____ DATE _____ 19__

| QUAN-TITY | ARTICLE AND DESCRIPTION | NUMBER WEIGHT | UNIT PRICE | AMOUNT | |
|---|---|---|---|---|---|
| | | | | | |
| | | | | | |
| | | | | | |
| | | | | | |
| | | | | | |
| | | | | | |
| | | | | | |
| | | | | | |
| | | | | | |
| | | | | | |
| | | | | | |
| | | | | | |
| | | | | | |
| | | | | | |
| | | | | | |
| | | | | | |
| | | | | | |
| | | | | | |
| | | | | | |
| | | | | | |

Head of Department

**Figure 6.2** A form that could be used like a requisition for inter-kitchen transfers if an establishment has more than one kitchen.

| | EMPLOYEES CAFETERIA COST RECORD | | | | |
|---|---|---|---|---|---|
| MONTH: | | | | | |
| | EMPLOYEES CAFETERIA | | | | |
| DATE | STORES ISSUES | KITCHEN TRANSFERS | TOTAL AVAILABLE | LESS CASH SALES | TOTAL COST |
| 1 | | | | | |
| 2 | | | | | |
| 3 | | | | | |
| 4 | | | | | |
| 5 | | | | | |
| 6 | | | | | |
| 7 | | | | | |
| 8 | | | | | |
| 9 | | | | | |
| 10 | | | | | |
| 11 | | | | | |
| 12 | | | | | |
| 13 | | | | | |
| 14 | | | | | |
| 15 | | | | | |
| 16 | | | | | |
| 17 | | | | | |
| 18 | | | | | |
| 19 | | | | | |
| 20 | | | | | |
| 21 | | | | | |
| 22 | | | | | |
| 23 | | | | | |
| 24 | | | | | |
| 25 | | | | | |
| 26 | | | | | |
| 27 | | | | | |
| 28 | | | | | |
| 29 | | | | | |
| 30 | | | | | |
| 31 | | | | | |
| Total | | | | | |

**Figure 6.3** A form that could be used for calculating daily cost of employee meals if the establishment has an employee cafeteria.

*Net Food Cost*

Once all the preceding columns have been filled in, Net Food Cost for the day can be calculated, as follows:

$$
\begin{array}{c}
\text{Storeroom issues} \\
+ \\
\text{Direct purchases} \\
+ \\
\text{Transfers in} \\
- \\
\text{Transfers out} \\
- \\
\text{Employee meals} \\
= \\
\text{Net food cost today}
\end{array}
$$

The Net Food Cost To Date figure is the sum of today's and all the preceding days' Net Food Cost Today figures. In other words, it is an accumulated food cost amount.

*Sales*

The Sales Today figure is entered from the sales records and the Sales To Date figure is calculated in the same way as the accumulated food cost. With this information, food cost percentages, both daily and accumulated, can be calculated.

*Food Cost Percentage*

The equation for calculating food cost percentage is

$$
\frac{\text{Food cost}}{\text{Food sales}} \times 100 = \text{Food Cost} \%
$$

This same equation applies whether we are calculating a daily figure or an accumulated one. For example, the day 2 daily food cost percentage is

$$
\frac{\$\,337.21}{\$1,251.70} \times 100 = 26.9\%
$$

and the to date food cost percentage is

$$
\frac{\$\,720.94}{\$2,361.85} \times 100 = 30.5\%
$$

Note that on day 3, because it was a Sunday, there were no direct purchases. As a result, the Food Cost % Today figure is very low. The accumulated percentage is also reduced considerably.

## MONTH-END ADJUSTMENTS

At the month-end, two adjustments to the Net Food Cost To Date figure are required: (1) storeroom inventory difference, and (2) open stock inventory level change.

### Storeroom Inventory Difference Adjustment

If the actual inventory is *greater* than our receiving report summary Closing Inventory, then the difference is *subtracted*; if actual inventory is *lower*, then the difference is *added* to the month-end Net Food Cost To Date. In the illustration (Figure 6.1), the actual inventory was lower; therefore we added the difference of $26.91 to the food cost.

The $26.91 is added because at the month-end we discovered that *actual* inventory value (as a result of a physical stock-taking) was less than we thought it was (according to the last day of the month Closing Inventory figure on the receiving report summary). The assumption is that items must have been issued from the storeroom without a requisition, or that pricing, extension, or addition errors were made on requisitions during the month. This "shortage" in inventory is treated as if it were another requisition, and thus becomes a further addition to Net Food Cost. If actual inventory at month-end is greater than the receiving report summary Closing Inventory figure on the last day of the month, the difference is subtracted from Net Food Cost. In this case, the assumption is that requisitions must have been overpriced and/or overadded during the month.

### Open Stock Inventory Level Change Adjustment

As mentioned in the previous chapter, there is always an amount of food in production that has not yet been used and sold. If at the month-end this open stock is *higher* than that for the previous month, we *subtract* the difference; if it is *lower*, we *add* the difference to our month-end Net Food Cost To Date. In this illustration (Figure 6.1), the open stock was higher; therefore we subtracted the difference of $420.

Our month-end food cost percentage can now be calculated as follows:

$$\frac{\$\,9{,}197.89}{\$31{,}897.30} \times 100 = 28.84\%$$

## ACCURACY OF DAILY FOOD COST PERCENTAGE

By itself, the *daily* food cost percentage is often not an accurate indicator. Most food purchases that do not go into stores are charged directly to production (food cost), and on a day of heavy purchases (prior to a holiday weekend, for example) the food cost percentage calculation may be too high to be balanced off for the next two or three days when little or no purchases are made. This is particularly so in the case of meat, which may only be purchased once a week. These peaks and valleys do not show up in the to date figures, which are averages for the period. The average figure is therefore more meaningful. If more accuracy is desired in the daily food cost, it can be obtained by "spreading" purchases or, in the case of meat, using a system of meat tags.

### Spreading Purchases

If, on a day of heavy deliveries, it is known that the purchases will not be used up on that day, the dollar amount can be spread over the next few days. For example, only $200 of a heavy $600 direct purchase can be shown on the daily food receiving report for that day, and the balance of $400 recorded in two $200 amounts on the two following days. Although this requires additional work and careful notations on invoices — and still does not guarantee an accurate daily food cost percentage — it will at least reduce the otherwise wide fluctuations in daily food cost percentage calculations.

### Meat Tags

In most food establishments, meat is the item that takes the largest slice of the purchase dollar. Since meat purchased in bulk is usually put into unlocked refrigerators or freezers close to the production kitchens rather than in a locked storeroom, some control needs to be exercised over it. One way to do this, *and* have greater accuracy in the calculation of the daily food cost percentage, is to use a system of *meat tags*.

As shown in Figure 6.4, each meat tag is sequentially prenumbered. Each tag has two sections, separated by a perforation, that contain identical information. When meat is received, a meat tag for each separate cut must be made out by the receiver. The relevant information is copied from the invoice. The meat tag is then separated along the perforation; the top half is attached to the meat, and the bottom half is attached to the invoice.

With this system, even though meat is not put into the storeroom, the receiver, insofar as the daily food receiving report is concerned, treats the *invoice* as if it were. In other words, the amount of the invoice is recorded in the Storeroom column. In

MEAT TAG        #3743

Date _____ Nov. 1 _____

Supplier _____ J.J Joseph _____

Cut _____ Beef Ribs _____

Weight _____ 35 lb. _____

Cost/lb. _____ $1.83 _____

Total value _____ $64.05 _____

- - - - - - - - - - - - - - - - - -

MEAT TAG        #3743

Date _____ Nov. 1 _____

Supplier _____ J.J. Joseph _____

Cut _____ Beef Ribs _____

Weight _____ 35 lb. _____

Cost/lb. _____ $1.83 _____

Total value _____ $64.05 _____

**Figure 6.4** Meat tags help control meat, and can be an aid in calculating a more accurate daily food cost percentage figure.

the control office, the bottom half of each meat tag should be checked against the invoice for correctness of information. This part of the tag can then be filed in a box, in number sequence.

As meat is removed by the steward or kitchen staff to be put into production, the half of the tag attached to the meat is removed and put into a box with a slit in the top (a locked box would be preferable). Each day the control office collects these parts of the tags and treats them as if they were requisitions for

| RECONCILIATION OF MEAT TAGS | | | |
|---|---|---|---|
| MONTH | | | |
| DATE RECEIVED | TAG NUMBER | NAME OF ITEM | DATE ISSUED |
| | | | |
| | | | |
| | | | |
| | | | |
| | | | |
| | | | |
| | | | |
| | | | |
| | | | |
| | | | |
| | | | |
| | | | |
| | | | |
| | | | |
| | | | |
| | | | |
| | | | |
| | | | |
| | | | |
| | | | |

**Figure 6.5**  A form that could be used for recording meat tags day by day as they are received in the control office.

items issued from stores. In other words, the total dollar amount on the top halves of the tags is added to the total of "normal" requisitions from stores and that total is entered in the Storeroom Issues column of the receiving report summary sheet.

The corresponding bottom halves of the meat tags can now be removed from the filing box in the control office. At any time there should be meat in the refrigerators or freezers with top halves of tags still attached matching up with the bottom halves still in the filing box in the control office.

### Temperatures

Because of the high costs involved in purchases of meat and other refrigerated items and their perishable nature, some control over the temperature in refrigerator/freezer areas must be exercised. A refrigerator temperature report completed daily at various times during the day will show whether the equipment is in continuously good working order, thus keeping to a minimum the risk of food spoilage.

Humidity also plays a role in refrigeration. Too little relative humidity will dry out foods, too high relative humidity encourages spoilage. Guidelines for both temperature and relative humidity of some categories of food items are given below:

| Category | Temperature $°F$ | Temperature $°C$ | Relative Humidity % |
|----------|------------------|------------------|---------------------|
| Meat | 30-35 | $-1$-2 | 75-85 |
| Dairy items | 35-45 | 2-7 | 75-85 |
| Fruit and vegetables | 40-45 | 4-7 | 85-95 |
| Other items | 35-40 | 2-4 | 75-85 |

Frozen foods should generally be stored at a temperature between $-10°$ F and $+5°$ F.

## SUMMARY

Each day the control office should check the preceding day's daily food receiving report, invoices, and requisitions. Invoices should be spot-checked for prices and verified for correct extensions and additions. They should be correctly listed on the daily food receiving report, and that report should be checked for correct column additions. Requisitions should be spot-checked for cost of items and extensions and additions verified.

When this has been done, the relevant information can be transferred from the daily food receiving report and requisitions on to the appropriate columns of the receiving report summary. In this way, a running balance of storeroom inventory can be calculated each day, and at the month-end, this figure can be compared with the actual storeroom inventory. The figures may not be identical, but as long as they are close it will indicate that there is good control over storeroom food items.

The receiving report summary can be used to calculate a daily Net Food Cost (Storeroom Issues + Direct Purchases + Transfers In − Transfers Out − Employee Meals = Net Food Cost). Accumulation of the daily Net Food Costs gives Net Food Cost To Date.

The daily and to date Net Food Cost figures can be converted into food cost percentages when divided by the related Sales and multiplied by 100. The final month-end food cost percentage can then be calculated, after adjustments to Net Food Cost To Date have been made for (1) storeroom inventory difference and (2) open stock inventory level change.

More accuracy in the calculation of the daily food cost percentage can be obtained if purchases of bulk items of direct purchases are "spread" over a number of daily food receiving reports. The use of meat tags will serve this same purpose, and will also give better control over meat, which is not controlled through the storeroom. Because of the high cost of meat and related items, control over the temperature of the areas where they are stored must be exercised.

## DISCUSSION QUESTIONS

1. What is the control office procedure each day for checking the daily receiving report?

2. What two purposes are served by the receiving report summary?

3. On the receiving report summary, how is Closing Inventory calculated?

4. Give examples of the types of things that would require entries in the Transfers In and Transfers Out columns of the receiving report summary.

5. On the receiving report summary, how is the amount of Net Food Cost Today calculated?

6. What is the equation for calculating food cost percentage?

7. At the month-end, to arrive at a more accurate food cost percentage, two adjustments are required. What are these adjustments, and why are they necessary?

8. Describe briefly how the use of meat tags can aid in control.

## MULTIPLE CHOICE/DISCUSSION QUESTIONS

1. On the receiving report summary, Net Food Cost Today is calculated as follows:
   a. Storeroom Issues − Direct Purchases + Transfers In − Transfers Out + Employee Meals
   b. Storeroom Issues + Direct Purchases − Transfers In + Transfers Out + Employee Meals
   c. Storeroom Issues + Direct Purchases + Transfers In − Transfers Out + Employee Meals
   d. Storeroom Issues + Direct Purchases + Transfers In − Transfers Out − Employee Meals
   e. Using some other equation

2. If our month-end actual inventory figure is lower than the month-end Closing Inventory figure on the receiving report summary, the difference is
   a. Ignored.
   b. Added to the Opening Inventory figure at the beginning of next month.
   c. Subtracted from the Net Food Cost Today figure for that date.
   d. Added to the Net Food Cost To Date month-end figure.
   e. Added to the open stock inventory amount.

3. In many food establishments it is difficult to have an accurate daily food cost percentage because
   a. Too many errors are made on invoices and/or requisitions.
   b. Items included in the food cost for the day are not used up that day.
   c. There is not enough time for the control office to calculate it.
   d. Food inventory is usually taken only once a month.
   e. The accounting department is closed on Sundays.

## PROBLEMS

1. The receiving report summary gave the following information:

| | |
|---|---|
| Month-end Closing Inventory | $ 4,200 |
| Month-end Net Food Cost To Date | 18,100 |
| Month-end Sales To Date | 57,500 |

Other information:

| | |
|---|---|
| Actual inventory | $ 4,275 |
| Previous open stock inventory | 3,450 |
| Present open stock inventory | 3,525 |

*Calculate*    a. The Adjusted Month-End Food Cost
               b. The Month-End Food Cost Percentage

2. The Rich Recipe Restaurant has food sales for the month of $37,500. Its month-end food cost percentage is 40. At the beginning of the month, its food inventory was $4,850. At the end of the month its food inventory was $5,150. What was the inventory turnover rate for the month?

3. On June 9 the following figures, among others, appeared on the receiving report summary:

| | |
|---|---|
| Closing Inventory | $1,543.27 |
| Net Food Cost To Date | 1,279.18 |
| Sales To Date | 4,655.92 |

On June 10 the Storeroom Purchases and the Direct Purchases figures can be obtained by reference to the daily food receiving report for that day. This information can be taken from the solution to Problem 1, Chapter 4. Requisitions for June 10 totaled $44.52, and this total included a requisition for items sent from food stores to the cocktail lounge, $8.33. On June 10 wine was received from the bar for cooking purposes, $4.30; bar supplies (syrup, fruit) were sent from the kitchen to the bar, $8.16. Employee meals on June 10 are estimated to be $15.50. Food sales on June 10: $481.40.

From all the above information, complete the entries for each of the following receiving report summary columns for June 10:

Opening Inventory
Storeroom Purchases
Storeroom Issues
Closing Inventory
Direct Purchases

Transfers In
Transfers Out
Employee Meals
Net Food Cost Today
Net Food Cost To Date
Sales Today
Sales To Date
Food Cost % Today
Food Cost % To Date

4. On August 30 the following figures, among others, appeared on the receiving report summary:

| | |
|---|---|
| Closing Inventory | $ 1,758.45 |
| Net Food Cost To Date | 9,119.60 |
| Sales To Date | 23,206.05 |

On August 31 the Storeroom Purchases and Direct Purchases figures can be taken from the daily food receiving report for that date. This information can be obtained from the solution to Problem 2, Chapter 4.

Requisitions dated August 31 totaled $85.91 for items issued from the food storeroom. Included in this amount was $10.43 for items delivered to the kitchen *after* inventory was taken at month-end. Change the date on this requisition to September 1 and exclude it from your Storeroom Issues for August 31. Also included in the total of $85.91 are items issued from food stores to the cocktail lounge, $15.49. Staff meals are estimated to be $53.75.

The actual inventory of food stores on August 31 was $1,784.48. However, on checking through the daily food receiving report for August 31, you notice that one delivery in the amount of $35.15 (soft drinks from Liquid Bottlers) had been put into the storeroom *after* the actual inventory had been taken. Adjust the actual inventory figure accordingly.

Sales on August 31 were $901.10. It is estimated that kitchen open stock inventory on August 31 was $1,300; on July 31 it had been estimated at $1,200.

a. Complete the receiving report summary for August 31.
b. Calculate the adjusted month-end food cost and month-end food cost percentage.

5. On September 30, the daily food receiving report gave the following information:

| | |
|---|---|
| Direct Purchases | $451.67 |
| Storeroom Purchases | 175.90 |

However, on checking the report, the following adjustments need made:

a. The Storeroom column total included an invoice for $25.20 which should have been recorded in the Direct Purchases column. Correct these column totals.

b. The Storeroom column included an invoice in the amount of $43.55 for goods received after the September month-end actual inventory had been taken. The date on this invoice is going to be changed to October 1, and it will be recorded on the daily food receiving report for that date. Change the September 30 report accordingly.

c. A delivery was made on September 30 in the amount of $27.20 for which no invoice had been received. A memorandum invoice was made up by the receiver, but he forgot to record it on the daily food receiving report. The items were put into the storeroom.

The following additional information is required for completion of the receiving report summary for September 30:

a. Opening Inventory, $2,576.98.

b. Storeroom Issues, $135.21. Note, however, that this total included food items amounting to $52.87 which were requisitioned by departments other than the food department. On checking the additions of the requisitions for September 30, you notice that one of them, for items issued to the kitchen, had been underadded by $10. Further, you have on hand a requisition dated October 1. It had been dated October 1 by the storekeeper because the goods were issued to the kitchen subsequent to month-end stock-taking. However, the food was used by the kitchen on September 30. This requisition totaled $31.48 and must be added to the Storeroom Issues for the day (given above). Note that the actual inventory total (given below) must also be adjusted for this transaction.

c. There were no Transfers In on September 30.

d. Transfers Out must include $12.62 for items transferred from the kitchen to the lounge on the last day of September.

e. Employee Meals are estimated at $10 on this day.

f. Net Food Cost for the period September 1-29, $12,749.32.

g. Sales, September 1-29, $32,149.50.

h. Sales, September 30, $1,412.35.

*Required:* a. Complete the receiving report summary for September 30 and calculate the Food Cost % Today and the Food Cost % To Date.

b. Calculate the Adjusted Month-end Food Cost and Month-end Food Cost Percentage given the following additional information: actual inventory (before any necessary adjustments), $2,669.50; open stock estimate August 31, $2,250; open stock estimate September 30, $2,075.

c. Comment on any of the results obtained.

# 7

# Food Production

## Objectives

After studying this chapter, the reader will be able to

1. Contrast the value of a food cost percentage with food cost expressed only in dollars.

2. List the five steps in the cycle of food cost control.

3. List the three factors that influence the food cost percentage of an individual menu item.

4. Calculate potential cost and potential cost percentage.

5. Complete a market cost index form and use the information to adjust an establishment's potential food cost percentage.

6. Write a one- or two-sentence explanation of the need for standard recipes and portion sizes.

7. Complete a butchering and cooking test form and use the information provided by a completed form.

8. Use cost factors to calculate menu item costs.

9. Explain why a supplier's price to you for meat, although the lowest of any, may not be the most advantageous.

10. Calculate menu item selling prices given the menu item cost and the desired food cost percentage.

The kitchen (production) areas pose the greatest problem insofar as control of food cost is concerned. There are certain production control techniques available for use in special situations (these will be discussed later), but the physical impossibility of tracing each item of food through the receiving, storage, and production areas, and verifying its sale, is apparent.

For this reason, *food cost percentage* has been developed over the years as a useful yardstick; with the implementation of basic control procedures in all areas, it is one of management's methods of determining whether or not it is making an adequate gross profit on food sales. Why the emphasis on a percentage figure? Simply because it is easier to compare a percentage than it is to compare absolute dollars of costs.

|  | This Month | Last Month |
|---|---|---|
| Sales | $70,000 | $50,000 |
| Food cost | 31,500 | 20,000 |

It is difficult to tell from these figures if food cost has gone up more than it should have in proportion to sales. But if we convert

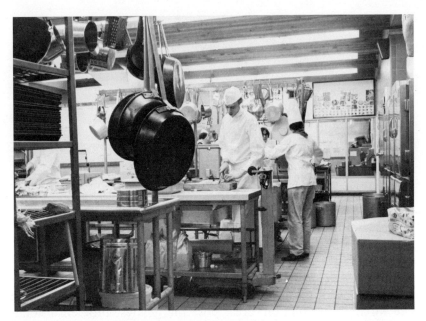

**Figure 7.1** The kitchen and other food production areas require some specialized controls because of the difficulty of trying to keep track of every food item from purchasing through production areas to the sales departments. British Columbia Government Photo.

the figures to percentages, we can quickly see that, in relation to sales, food cost is much higher this month than last.

|                | This Month | Last Month |
|----------------|:----------:|:----------:|
| Food cost %    | 45.0       | 40.0       |

## THE CONTROL CYCLE

The objective in food cost control is to compare the actual food cost percentage for a period (a day, a week, a month) with a *potential* food cost percentage—potential being what management thinks it should have, or what is desired. The steps in the control cycle are these:

1. Set a potential food cost percentage that is desirable and attainable.
2. Establish standard recipes and portion sizes.
3. Calculate menu item costs.

4. Determine the selling prices of the menu items.

5. Periodically evaluate the actual results obtained.

## 1. SET A POTENTIAL FOOD COST PERCENTAGE

The basic equation for expressing food cost as a percentage is

$$\frac{\text{Food cost}}{\text{Food sales}} \times 100$$

There is no ideal percentage that an operator should try to achieve. Food cost percentage can be as low as 20 percent or as high as 60 percent, and at both ends of the scale the operators could be as successful as those whose food cost percentage is somewhere in between. The food cost percentage of individual menu items can be influenced by any or all of these factors:

1. The raw cost of the food

2. The portion size served

3. The selling price

For example, if food cost prices go up and you do not want to change the quality of what you serve or the selling price, then a reduction of the portion size may be the way to achieve the same food cost percentage prevailing before costs went up.

The food cost percentage is also affected by the use of convenience foods. An establishment purchasing its meat in bulk and doing its own butchering may have a food cost of 40 percent and a labor cost of 30 percent. By switching its purchases of meat to convenience, preportioned items and eliminating the need for an on-premises butcher, food cost may go up to 45 percent and labor cost may decline to 25 percent. Thus, comparison of food cost percentages between two establishments, one of which uses more convenience foods than the other, is difficult.

### Quantity Sold

Since individual menu items have different costs and selling prices and different cost percentages, in order to calculate overall food cost percentage we must take into consideration the *quantity* sold, or expected to be sold, of each menu item. (The ratio of what we sell of each menu item is known as the *sales mix* and will be discussed at greater length in the next chapter).

In a new operation, it is obviously almost impossible to predict exactly how many of each item customers are going to buy. But in an ongoing concern, we can analyze sales on a menu item tally sheet (see Figure 7.2) and use this information to calculate the overall potential food cost percentage for the future. As long a period as possible should be included in the analysis (preferably a month). Once menu item sales have been tallied, the quantities can be transferred to a test period potential cost form (see Figure 7.3).

On this form, Quantity Sold x Item Cost gives us Total Cost; and Quantity Sold x Item Sale gives us Total Sales. The Total Cost column total divided by the Total Sales column total and multiplied by 100 equals the potential food cost percentage. Once this potential percentage has been calculated, it can be altered by changing cost prices (changing supplier or changing quality), changing selling prices, or changing portion sizes of certain menu items. Alternatively, menu items could be added to or taken off the menu, or an attempt could be made to change the quantity of various menu items sold. Once a satisfactory percentage has been achieved, and as long as menu item cost and selling prices do not change and the sales mix stays relatively the same as during the test period, the *actual* food cost percentage in future periods should be close to the calculated potential food cost percentage.

| MENU ITEM TALLY SHEET | | Date _August_ | |
|---|---|---|---|
| Item | Sold | | Total |
| Shrimp Cocktail | 7HL 7HL 7HL 7HL | 7HL / | 1941 |
| Onion Soup | 7HL 7HL 7HL 7HL | // | 1462 |
| Sirloin Steak | 7HL 7HL 7HL 7HL | | 541 |
| Prime Rib | 7HL 7HL 7HL 7HL | | 767 |
| Roast Veal | 7HL 7HL 7HL 7HL | | 315 |
| | | | 611 |

**Figure 7.2** Sales of all menu items can be easily summarized on a menu item tally sheet.

| TEST PERIOD POTENTIAL COST | | | | | Period _August_ | | |
|---|---|---|---|---|---|---|---|
| Item | Quantity Sold | Item Cost | Item Sale | Cost % | Total Cost | Sales | |
| Shrimp Cocktail | 1941 | 0.42 | 1.45 | 29.0 | 815.22 | 2814.45 | |
| Onion Soup | 1462 | 0.16 | 0.75 | 21.3 | 233.92 | 1096.50 | |
| Sirloin steak | 541 | 3.26 | 7.95 | 41.0 | 1763.66 | 4300.95 | |
| Prime rib | 767 | 2.43 | 6.95 | 35.0 | 1863.81 | 5330.65 | |
| Roast beef | 315 | 2.50 | 6.95 | 36.5 | 800.10 | 2189.25 | |
| | | | | | | | |
| | | | | | | | |
| | | | | Totals | 9315.49 | 31,248.30 | |

Potential Cost Percent $= \dfrac{\text{Total Cost}}{\text{Total Sales}} \times 100 = \dfrac{9315.49}{31248.30} \times 100 = 29.8\%$

**Figure 7.3** The potential cost percentage can be calculated by analyzing the sales during a test period.

## Market Cost Index

In these days of rising costs, however, it is highly unlikely that all other things will remain equal, and it may be necessary to repeat the test cycle fairly regularly to recalculate the potential. Another, much quicker, way to recalculate the potential is to use a market cost index (see Figure 7.4).

During the initial test period, a dozen or more key purchase items are listed. Quantities used during this test period are multiplied by their test period cost. When costs are known to be rising, the new costs can be inserted and multiplied by test period quantities. We can then use this information to recalculate our potential cost percentage, with the following equation:

$$\begin{array}{ccc} \text{Test period} & \times & \dfrac{\text{New period total cost}}{\text{Test period total cost}} = \dfrac{\text{New Period}}{\text{Potential cost \%}} \\ \text{Potential cost \%} & & \end{array}$$

$$29.8\% \quad \times \quad \dfrac{\$3,211.36}{\$3,124.40} \quad = \quad 30.7\%$$

| MARKET COST INDEX | | | | Test period _August_ | | New Period _____ | |
|---|---|---|---|---|---|---|---|
| Item | Quantity Used | Test Period | | New Period: _Nov._ | | New Period | |
| | | Unit Cost | Total Cost | Unit Cost | Total Cost | Unit Cost | Total Cost |
| _Bacon_ | 75 lb | 1.30 | 97.50 | 1.35 | 101.25 | | |
| _Butter_ | 394 lb | 0.85 | 334.90 | 0.90 | 354.60 | | |
| _Coffee_ | 307 lb | 0.97 | 297.79 | 0.95 | 291.65 | | |
| _Shrimps_ | 270 lb | 3.25 | 877.50 | 3.30 | 891.00 | | |
| | | | | | | | |
| Totals | | | 3,124.40 | | 3211.36 | | |

**Figure 7.4** The market cost index can be used to readjust the potential cost percentage in times of changing cost prices.

## 2. ESTABLISH STANDARD RECIPES AND PORTION SIZES

A _standard recipe_ is simply a written formula detailing the quantities of each ingredient required to produce a certain quantity and quality of a particular menu item. The formula also includes a description of the cooking method to be followed to achieve a desired quality. A _portion size_ is the quantity of any menu item to be served each customer. The standard recipe should therefore also include the portion size.

If for no other reason than customer satisfaction, standard recipes should be prepared for all menu items. All those involved in food preparation should be instructed to follow these recipes and serve constant portions so that returning customers will know what to expect. Standard recipes are also necessary so that the cost can be calculated accurately for each separate menu item. Without standard recipes, or if standard recipes are not followed, costs cannot be properly controlled.

If recipes call for a certain weight of meat per portion, then portion scales should be provided so that the quantity can be checked frequently. Casserole dishes of predetermined size and specific size serving spoons and ladles are also of use in portion control. It should be pointed out to the staff involved that a 1 oz additional amount served on a basic 10 oz portion of meat may seem insignificant, but the same error made on every portion served will cause the food cost on that item to be 10 percent higher than it should be—and that _is_ significant.

**Figure 7.5** Portion scales are indispensable and help ensure that portion sizes are being followed. The model illustrated has a maximum 2 lb capacity, is graduated by 1/4 oz, and is accurate to 1/8 oz. Photograph courtesy Pelouze Scale Company, Evanston, Illinois.

Establishing portion sizes for all menu items can also be useful to the purchasing personnel and the kitchen production staff. For example, in anticipation of a certain number of customers at a banquet, the quantity of food to be purchased can be more accurately calculated and the kitchen staff will know how much to adjust ingredient amounts to prepare a given dish in sufficient quantity. Overproduction and possible wastage can be reduced.

One of the functions of the control office is to spot-check to see that recipes and portion sizes are being followed. In order to do this, control office staff must have copies of all recipes currently in use (a sample recipe form is illustrated in Figure 7.6). When testing portion sizes the control form illustrated in Figure 7.7 may be used instead of the individual recipe cards. The portion

| | RECIPE FORM | RECIPE FOR Ground Beef Stew | | | | | | | |
|---|---|---|---|---|---|---|---|---|---|

**RECIPE FORM**   RECIPE FOR _Ground Beef Stew_

RECIPE NO. _32_

PORTION SIZE ___8 oz.___ _Dining_ ___ ROOM

QUANTITY PRODUCED 100 portions (8 oz)   PORTION SIZE ___8 oz.___ _Banquet_ ___ ROOM

| UNIT | INGREDIENTS | DATE: **Oct.** | | DATE: | | DATE: | | DATE: | |
|---|---|---|---|---|---|---|---|---|---|
| | | AT | AMOUNT | AT | AMOUNT | AT | AMOUNT | AT | AMOUNT |
| 15 | lb. ground beef | 1.20 | 18.00 | | | | | | |
| 1 | lb. flour | 0.15 | 0.15 | | | | | | |
| 4 | oz. tomato paste | 0.03 | 0.12 | | | | | | |
| 1 | gall. beef stock | C.30 | 0.30 | | | | | | |
| 1 | gall. brown stock | 0.20 | 0.20 | | | | | | |
| 4 | lb. fresh carrots - diced | 0.10 | 0.40 | | | | | | |
| | lb. fresh onions - diced | 0.04 | 0.24 | | | | | | |
| 2 | lb. celery - diced | 0.15 | 0.30 | | | | | | |
| 4 | lb. dehydrated green peas | 0.10 | 0.40 | | | | | | |
| | choped parsley, seasoning | | 0.05 | | | | | | |
| | | | | | | | | | |
| | | | | | | | | | |
| | | | | | | | | | |
| | Total Cost | | 20.16 | | | | | | |
| | | | | | | | | | |
| | Cost per portion | | 20¢ | | | | | | |
| | | | | | | | | | |

PREPARATION AND SERVICE

1. Brown meat in saucepan or electric frying pan
2. Add flour and tomato paste and mix well
3. Add beef and brown stocks - simmer approximately 1 hour
4. Add carrots, onions, and celery - cook until tender
5. Add dehydrated peas and parsley and seasoning
6. Serve in 8 oz. casserole dish with curry dumpling

**Figure 7.6** Recipe forms should be drawn up for all items on the menu.

| | STANDARD PORTION SIZES | | Date | October 197- |
|---|---|---|---|---|
| Item | Dining Room | | Coffee Shop | Banquet |
| | A la carte | Table d'hôte | | |
| Sirloin steak | 10 oz. | 8 oz. | 8 oz. | |
| Prime rib | 10 oz. | 8 oz. | | 6 oz. |
| Filet mignon, sm. | 6 oz. | 5 oz. | 5 oz. | 5 oz. |
| Filet mignon, lge. | 8 oz. | 7 oz. | | |
| Lobster tail | 8 oz. | | | |
| Salmon steak | 8 oz. | 6 oz. | 6 oz. | 6 oz. |
| Filet of sole | 8 oz. | | | |
| | | | | |

**Figure 7.7** The standard portion sizes form will advise staff involved of the portion sizes currently in effect.

size form will list all menu items offered in the various sales areas and show the portion size(s) currently in effect.

## 3. CALCULATE MENU ITEM COSTS

Once recipes have been drawn up and portion sizes determined, portions can be costed. Usually this information can be incorporated into the recipe form (Figure 7.6). The beef stock, brown stock, and curry dumpling called for in the recipe in Figure 7.6 would have their own individual recipe forms and cost calculations. As can be seen, our cost per portion of ground beef stew, including dumpling, is calculated to be $0.20. As the cost of ingredients changes, so does portion cost. (The three sets of columns at the right on the recipe form are reserved for cost changes.) In some cases, the cost per portion needs to be increased to cover wastage of one kind or another. This wastage factor could add as much as 5 percent to the basic portion cost.

### Costing Problems

In some cases, costing portions requires more detailed calculations than those shown in the recipe form for ground beef stew. Consider the case of a restaurant that features roast beef on its menu. It uses trimmed, boneless, ready-to-cook top round, which it purchases in 5 lb quantities at $1.50 per pound. Cooking loss (dripping, evaporation) is 20 percent, and 4-oz medium-done *cooked* portions are served. What is the cost per portion?

| | |
|---|---|
| Total purchase cost | 5 lb x $1.50 = $7.50 |
| Cooking loss 20% | 1 lb |
| Net yield | 4 lb x 16 oz = 64 oz |

$$64 \text{ oz will provide } \frac{64}{4} = 16 \text{ portions}$$

$$\text{Portion cost } \frac{\$7.50}{16} = \$0.4688 \text{ or } 47\cancel{c}$$

To this must be added (on the recipe form) the cost of other items served with the roast, including garnish, to arrive at total menu item cost.

### Cooking Loss and Trimming

Any recipes in which weight loss in cooking is likely to occur should include the cooking temperature. For example, a medium-done roast beef cooked at 230°F (110°C) can have a weight loss of up to 15 percent. The same medium-done roast cooked at 360°F (182°C) will give a weight loss of well over 20 percent.

If meat is purchased unbutchered and is subject to trim loss (bones, fat) and/or weight loss in cooking, a butchering and cooking test form like that shown in Figure 7.8 will be useful. Trim and cooking loss tests should be carried out on a number of items of the same type and weight so that any variations in loss can then be averaged out. The illustration shows that our butchering and cooking test on prime rib gives us a cost of $0.138 per ounce before cooking, and $0.165 per ounce after cooking. Depending on whether a particular recipe called for a portion size to be costed out before or after cooking, we would use one or the other of these two unit cost prices.

### Cost Factors

It is useful to calculate and record the "cost factor(s)" on the butchering and cooking test form. The advantage of doing this is that if the supplier's price per pound changes, we do not have to retest and recalculate to obtain a new cost for menu costing purposes. The general equation for developing a cost factor is

$$\frac{\text{Our calculated cost per lb}}{\text{Supplier's price per lb}} = \text{Cost factor}$$

*Cost factor before cooking:*

$$\frac{2.21}{2.00} = \$1.105$$

## BUTCHERING AND COOKING TEST FORM

NAME OF ITEM _Prime Rib_ _____ GRADE _Choice_ ____

PIECES _1_ WEIGHING _13_ LBS. _4_ OZ. AT _$2.00_ TOTAL _$26.50_

DATE _Oct. 15/19—_ _____ DEALER _Meats Unlimited_ _____

| ITEM | WEIGHT | | RATIO | COST | | |
|---|---|---|---|---|---|---|
| | LB. | OZ. | | TOTAL | LB. | OZ. |
| **RAW YIELD:** | | | | | | |
| INITIAL RAW WEIGHT | 13 | 4 | 100.0% | | | |
| LESS BONES FAT & TRIM | 1 | 4 | 9.4 | | | |
| SALEABLE RAW WEIGHT | 12 | 0 | 90.6 | 26 50 | 2 21 | 0.138¢ |
| BREAKDOWN | | | | | | |
| | | | | | | |
| | | | | | | |
| | | | | | | |
| TOTAL | | | | 26 50 | | |
| **COOKED YIELD:** | | | | | | |
| SALEABLE RAW WEIGHT | 12 | 0 | 90.6% | | | |
| SHRINKAGE | 2 | 0 | 15.1 | | | |
| SALEABLE COOKED WEIGHT | 10 | 0 | 75.5 | 26 50 | 2 65 | 0.1654 |
| | | | | | | |
| | | | | | | |
| | | | | | | |
| | | | | | | |
| | | | | | | |
| TOTAL | | | | 26 50 | | |

**RAW OR COOKED PORTION COST AND PORTION COST FACTOR**

| NAME OF DISH | PORTION SIZE | NO. OF PORTIONS | COST PER OUNCE | TOTAL COST | COST FACTOR |
|---|---|---|---|---|---|
| _Prime Rib of Beef_ | 10 oz. | 1 | 0 16½ | 1 65 | 0.825 |
| | 8 oz. | 1 | 0 16½ = | 1 32 | 0.66 |
| | 6 oz. | 1 | 0 16½ = | 0 99 | 0.495 |
| | | | | | |
| TOTAL | | | | | |
| | | SIGNED | _James Jones_ | | |

*Handwritten margin notes:*

26.50 ÷ 12

2.21 ÷ 16)

90.6 = 7.55
12

7.55
× 2
15.1

1.65
2.00 (step price)

1.32
2.00

99
2.00

**Figure 7.8** The butchering and cooking test form is useful for calculating portion costs on items subject to loss from trimming, boning, and cooking.

Using the example in Figure 7.8, our cost factor per pound of prime rib would be

$$\frac{\$2.65}{\$2.00} = 1.325$$

If the supplier now changes his price, we can use this cost factor of 1.325 to quickly calculate our *new cost per pound after butchering, trimming and cooking.* Suppose the supplier's price increases from \$2 to \$2.15; our calculated cost after butchering and trimming is obviously also going to increase:

$$\$2.15 \times 1.325 = \$2.85 \text{ per pound}$$

A cost factor could be calculated, using the same general formula, for a 10 oz portion of prime rib. The formula, however, will be slightly different than the one given above. It will be

$$\frac{\text{Our calculated cost per portion}}{\text{Supplier's price per lb}} = \text{Cost factor per portion}$$

Or, using Figure 7.8,

$$\frac{\$1.65}{\$2.00} = 0.825$$

And if the supplier's price goes up from \$2 to \$2.15, our new cost per 10 oz portion of prime rib will be

$$\$2.15 \times 0.825 = \$1.77 \text{ per portion}$$

It can thus be seen that recording these cost factor(s) on the butchering and cooking test form can considerably shorten the recalculation of menu item costs when the supplier's price changes.

### Lowest Net Cost

Butchering (trim) tests may even indicate that the supplier with the lowest price may not be offering the lowest *net* cost per pound. Comparison of the figures below shows that supplier A's price *appears* lower (\$2 vs. \$2.05), but after trimming, the net cost per pound is lower from supplier B (\$2.48 vs. \$2.50).

|  | Purchase weight | Price per lb | Weight after trim | Net cost per lb |
|---|---|---|---|---|
| Supplier A | 10 lb | $2.00 | 8 lb | $2.50 |
| Supplier B | 10 lb | $2.05 | 8¼ lb | $2.48 |

## By-Products

If butchering is done in the kitchen, there are often usable (salable) by-products in addition to fat and bones. In our case, Figure 7.9 shows a purchase of prime rib that has two by-products: short rib and hamburger.

Total cost of the purchase was $51.85, and our problem is to distribute that cost among the three separate items. They cannot all be costed out at the overall cost per pound purchase price of $1.70, for that would mean that prime rib would have an unusually low cost for menu pricing, and hamburger would have too high a cost. The by-products should be costed out at the price that would have been paid if they had been purchased separately. This information will be readily available from the supplier. Multiplying these costs by the weights of the items we have gives us the following

$$
\begin{array}{lll}
3\tfrac{1}{2}\text{ lb short rib @ } \$1.34 \text{ (market)} & = & \$4.69 \\
1\tfrac{1}{4}\text{ lb hamburger @ } \$0.92 \text{ (market)} & = & \underline{\phantom{0}1.15} \\
& & \$5.84
\end{array}
$$

Deducting $5.84 from the total cost of the initial purchase, $51.85, gives us the value to be assigned to prime rib—$46.01. (Note, on the top part of Figure 7.9, that we have to work upward from the total cost of $51.85 to arrive at the $46.01 to be assigned to prime rib.) Finally, $46.01 divided by the amount of prime rib before cooking, 18 ½ lb, gives us a precooked cost per pound of $2.49.

The cost per ounce figures can then be calculated for each separate item. In the case of prime rib, we can continue to the bottom half of the sheet and calculate the cooked cost per pound ($3.02) and per ounce ($0.189), and finally cost out our portions and calculate our cost factor per pound (1.776), and per portion (see bottom right hand column of Figure 7.9).

# BUTCHERING AND COOKING TEST FORM

NAME OF ITEM  *Prime Rib*  GRADE *Choice*
PIECES *1* WEIGHING *30* LBS. *8* OZ. AT *$1.70* Total *$51.85*
DATE *Oct. 21/19—*  DEALER *Mid West*

| ITEM | WEIGHT LB. | WEIGHT OZ. | RATIO | COST TOTAL | COST LB. | COST OZ. |
|------|----|----|-------|-------|-----|-----|
| RAW YIELD: | | | | | | |
| INITIAL RAW WEIGHT | 30 | 8 | 100.0% | | | |
| LESS BONES FAT & TRIM | 7 | 4 | 23.8 | | | |
| SALEABLE RAW WEIGHT | 23 | 4 | 76.2 | | | |
| BREAKDOWN | | | | | | |
| Prime Rib | 18 | 8 | 60.7 | 46 | 01 | 2 | 49 | 0.1564 |
| Short Rib | 3 | 8 | 11.5 | 4 | 69 | market 1 | 34 | 0.0844 |
| Hamburger | 1 | 4 | 4.0 | 1 | 15 | market 0 | 92 | 0.0584 |
| TOTAL | | | | 51 | 85 | | |
| COOKED YIELD: | | | | | | |
| SALEABLE RAW WEIGHT | 18 | 8 | 60.7 | | | |
| SHRINKAGE | 3 | 4 | 10.7 | | | |
| SALEABLE COOKED WEIGHT | 15 | 4 | 50.0 | 46 | 01 | 3 | 02 | 0.1894 |
| | | | | | | |
| | | | | | | |
| | | | | | | |
| TOTAL | | | | 46 | 01 | | |

RAW OR COOKED PORTION COST AND PORTION COST FACTOR

| NAME OF DISH | PORTION SIZE | NO. OF PORTIONS | COST PER OUNCE | TOTAL COST | COST FACTOR |
|------|------|------|------|------|------|
| Prime Rib | 10 oz. | 1 | 0 189 ¢ | 1 89 | 1.112 |
| | 8 oz. | 1 | 0 189 ¢ | 1 51 | 0.888 |
| | 6 oz. | 1 | 0 189 ¢ | 1 13 | 0.665 |
| TOTAL | | | | | |
| | | SIGNED | *James Jones* | | |

**Figure 7.9** Butchering and cooking test form for prime rib.

If the supplier's price goes up from $1.70 to $1.80, our new cost per pound (cooked) for prime rib will be $1.80 x 1.776 = $3.20 (instead of $3.02). If the supplier's price goes down to $1.60, our new cooked cost per pound for prime rib will be $1.60 x 1.776 = $2.84.

## Cost Factors for By-products

Cost factors can also be developed for the by-products. Although not shown on the butchering and cooking test form in Figure 7.9, they would be calculated as follows:

$$\frac{\text{Market price of by-product per lb}}{\text{Supplier's price including by-products per lb}} = \frac{\text{Cost factor for}}{\text{by-products}}$$

Short rib $\frac{\$1.34}{\$1.70} = 0.788$    Hamburger $\frac{\$0.92}{\$1.70} = 0.541$

If the supplier's price goes up to $1.80, we would then use the following new cost prices:

Short rib $1.80 x 0.788 = $1.42    Hamburger $1.80 x 0.541 = $0.97

And if the supplier's price goes down to $1.60

Short rib $1.60 x 0.788 = $1.26    Hamburger $1.60 x 0.541 = $0.87

Note that cost factors can be determined: per pound before cooking, per pound after cooking, or (as illustrated earlier), per portion.

## Alternative Costing Method

There is an alternative method for costing the prime ingredient and the by-products when purchasing meat in bulk and doing one's own butchering. To illustrate, let us assume we have purchased 40 lb of unbutchered meat at $1 per pound—a total cost of $40. After butchering, it yields the following cuts (no bones and no wastage):

20 lb  roast
10 lb  braising meat
10 lb  hamburger
40 lb  total

Our supplier advises us that if we had purchased each of

these cuts separately from him, already butchered, the prices per pound would have been:

| | |
|---|---|
| Roast | $1.75 |
| Braising meat | $1.00 |
| Hamburger | $0.50 |

Therefore, if we had purchased the meat already butchered, our total cost would have been not $40 but:

| | |
|---|---|
| 20 lb roast @ $1.75 lb | $35.00 |
| 10 lb braising meat @ $1.00 lb | 10.00 |
| 10 lb hamburger @ $0.50 lb | 5.00 |
| Total | $50.00 |

By doing our own butchering, our cost is $\$\frac{40.00}{50.00}$ or 4/5 (or 80 percent) of what it would otherwise be. If we apply this fraction (4/5) or percentage (80 percent) to the supplier's "already butchered" cost figures, we have the following:

| | |
|---|---|
| Roast | $1.75 x 4/5 (80%) = $1.40 |
| Braising meat | $1.00 x 4/5 (80%) = $0.80 |
| Hamburger | $0.50 x 4/5 (80%) = $0.40 |

These costs—$1.40, $0.80, and $0.40 for roast, braising meat, and hamburger, respectively—are *our* costs by purchasing in bulk and doing our own butchering. This can be easily proved by multiplying these costs by the quantities purchased to see if we do indeed arrive at a total cost of $40 (40 lb x $1).

| | | |
|---|---|---|
| Roast | 20 lb x $1.40 = | $28 |
| Braising meat | 10 lb x $0.80 = | $ 8 |
| Hamburger | 10 lb x $0.40 = | $ 4 |
| Total | | $40 |

Cost factors can be worked out in the usual manner. Using the equation

$$\frac{\text{Our calculated cost per lb}}{\text{Supplier's price per lb}} = \text{Cost factor}$$

we have the following:

|              |                         |
|--------------|-------------------------|
| Roast        | $1.40 ÷ $1.00 = 1.4     |
| Braising meat| $0.80 ÷ $1.00 – 0.8     |
| Hamburger    | $0.40 ÷ $1.00 = 0.4     |

If the supplier raises the price of the unbutchered cut from $1 to $1.20, our new cost per pound for each of the three cuts, using the already calculated cost factors, would be as follows:

|              |                          |
|--------------|--------------------------|
| Roast        | $1.20 x 1.4 = $1.68      |
| Braising meat| $1.20 x 0.8 = $0.96      |
| Hamburger    | $1.20 x 0.4 = $0.48      |

Although the method outlined in this section to calculate cost per pound of various cuts purchased in bulk and butchered on the premises might give costs that differ somewhat from the approach detailed in an earlier section, it is arithmetically just as accurate and in some ways more logical.

## 4. DETERMINE MENU ITEM SELLING PRICES

Once menu item costs have been calculated, selling prices must be determined. The easiest method is to use a cost multiplication factor. If, for example, a 40 percent food cost is desired, multiply the cost by 2 1/2. A list of some of the basic factors follows:

| Potential % Desired | Cost Multiplication Factor |
|---------------------|----------------------------|
| 20%                 | 5.00                       |
| 25                  | 4.00                       |
| 30                  | 3.33                       |
| 35                  | 2.86                       |
| 40                  | 2.50                       |
| 45                  | 2.22                       |
| 50                  | 2.00                       |

These cost multiplication factors are obtained by dividing the related percentage into 100 (for example, $100 ÷ 20 = 5$).

However, it may not be possible to apply the same multiplication factor to all items featured on the menu. Because of competition and customer resistance, some items may have to

be marked up less (using a lower multiplication factor) and thus
yielding a higher food cost percentage. These high-cost items can
be balanced by applying a high factor on other dishes that will
then yield a relatively low food cost percentage. Some items which
are served both as *table d'hôte* and *à la carte* may have two
different selling prices; or the same item sold in the coffee shop
may have a lower markup than in the dining room (where customers expect to pay more for more luxurious surroundings
and more service).

The potential food cost percentage established in step 1
is therefore only a starting point, a guide to establishing menu
selling prices. Step 5 in the food production control cycle is
periodically to evaluate the results obtained. This step will be
discussed in the next chapter.

## SUMMARY

Because of the difficulty of keeping track of each separate item
of food put into production, food cost percentage is used as a
general indicator of whether or not food costs are in line. A
percent figure is used because changes in food cost, relative to
sales, can be more quickly identified this way.

There are five basic steps to this control cycle.

1. *Set a potential food cost percentage that is desirable
and attainable.* This is only a starting point, because the food cost
percentage is contingent upon the cost of the food, the size of the
portion, and the menu selling price. It can also be affected by the
use of more, or fewer, convenience foods.

One of the major factors influencing the overall food cost
percentage is the *quantity* sold of each different menu item. This
is known as the *sales mix*. In a new food operation this can be
very difficult to forecast, thus making the potential food cost
percentage difficult to determine. In an on-going concern, however,
we can use information about what was sold in the past to calculate the potential food cost percentage for the future. Test
period results of what were sold can be summarized on a menu
item tally sheet. Then, on a test period potential cost form, these
quantities can be multiplied by the related menu item costs and
selling prices. Total cost divided by total sales and multiplied by

100 then gives us our potential cost percentage. As long as conditions (cost prices, selling prices, and the sales mix) remain the same, future actual cost percentage results should be the same as, or very close to, the potential cost percentage.

In periods of rising costs, the potential cost percentage should be revised upward from time to time (or downward if costs decline). A number of key food items used during the test period can be costed out by multiplying quantity used by unit cost. As costs change, these same quantities can be costed out using their new prices. The general equation for calculating the new period potential cost percentage is

$$\text{Test period potential cost \%} \quad \text{x} \quad \frac{\text{New period total cost}}{\text{Test period total cost}}$$

2. *Establish standard recipes and portion sizes.* Recipes detail the quantities of raw ingredients required to produce a certain number of portions, and spell out the cooking method to be used to achieve a desired quality. Standard recipes and portion sizes must be followed to control costs and to ensure consistency of product for customer satisfaction.

3. *Calculate menu item costs.* This is a relatively straightforward procedure in the case of many menu items, although the arithmetic can become a bit more involved when meat purchased is subject to losses from trimming, boning, and evaporation in cooking. It is necessary to calculate the cost per pound or ounce after loss tests have been conducted and the net yield of salable meat is known. When on-premise butchering gives salable by-products, these will have to be deducted, at market value, from the cost of the unbutchered meat in order to arrive at the net cost of the main item. One useful tool that can be developed from these calculations is the *cost factor.* The cost factor makes it very easy to recalculate menu item costs when the supplier's price changes. There is an alternative method for calculating costs of various cuts when meat is purchased in bulk and butchered on the premises. Although this method might give slightly different costs per pound for each different cut, it is, arithmetically, just as accurate and still permits calculation of cost factors in the usual way.

4. *Determine selling prices of menu items.* Once costs

have been calculated, selling prices can be determined. However, not all menu items will have the same individual markup and therefore not all items will give the same food cost percentage. Customer resistance and competitive pricing must be kept in mind. The objective is to strike a balance, with some items having a lower, and others a higher, food cost percentage than the overall average desired.

5. *Periodically evaluate the results obtained.* This step will be discussed in the next chapter.

## DISCUSSION QUESTIONS

1. Why is the food cost percentage more useful than knowing only the dollar amount of food cost?

2. What, according to the text, are the five steps in the food cost control cycle?

3. What three main factors can influence the food cost percentage of a particular menu item?

4. What are standard recipes and portion sizes? Why are they necessary?

5. Why does a change in the temperature at which some items are cooked have a bearing on the cost per portion served?

6. What is the purpose of calculating a cost factor per pound, per ounce, or per portion?

7. Why is it not always advantageous to purchase meat items at the lowest price available?

8. List some of the basic cost multiplication factors for calculating menu selling prices to give a specific cost percentage.

## MULTIPLE CHOICE/DISCUSSION QUESTIONS

1. The quantity we sell of each of the various menu items affects overall food cost percentage because

   a. The individual menu items have different costs.

b. The individual menu items have different selling prices.
c. The individual menu items have different markups.
d. The individual menu items have different cost percentages.
e. Any or all of the above are true.
f. None of the above is true.

2. In conducting butchering and cooking tests, a number of cuts of the same type and approximately the same weight should be used because

a. The temperature we cook at can influence meat shrinkage.
b. A different portion size of the same meat may be served in the dining room as opposed to a banquet.
c. Variations in loss from bone, trim, and cooking can be averaged out.
d. The *total* price for each of the several cuts will be different.
e. Some cuts will have by-products while others will not.

3. Not all menu items can be marked up to give the same food cost percentage because

a. They may all have different costs.
b. We must have a range of selling prices on the menu.
c. Suppliers' costs are constantly changing.
d. There is a choice of cost multiplication factors to arrive at selling prices and we should use a number of them.
e. Competition and customer acceptance must be kept in mind when determining menu selling prices.

## PROBLEMS

1. The Dandy Dining Room has the following menu item cost and selling prices; alongside the items are figures from a test period taken from a menu item tally sheet showing the various quantities sold.

| Menu Item | Item Cost | Item Selling Price | Test Period Quantity Sold |
|---|---|---|---|
| Half spring chicken | $0.94 | $2.95 | 1,326 |
| Salmon steak | 1.21 | 4.75 | 821 |
| Sirloin steak | 2.56 | 6.95 | 1,555 |
| Lobster Thermidor | 4.14 | 8.95 | 317 |
| Prime rib | 1.59 | 7.95 | 1,101 |

*Calculate*  a. The cost percentage for each of the five items.
b. The overall potential cost percentage for the Dandy Dining Room, assuming these are the only items on its menu.

2. A country club food department's potential food cost percentage has been

calculated, during a one-month test period, to be 33.5 percent. During this one month the following quantities of certain major purchases were used at the cost prices shown below:

| Item | Quantity Used | Cost Price |
|------|--------------|------------|
| Beef sides | 374 lb | $1.25 lb |
| Eggs | 220 doz | 0.85 doz |
| Sole filets | 89 lb | 0.90 lb |
| Coffee | 258 lb | 1.03 lb |
| Lobsters—whole | 108 | 3.25 each |
| Chickens | 293 lb | 0.69 lb |

Three months later, the invoices were checked for price changes, which were as follows:

| Item | New Cost Price |
|------|----------------|
| Beef sides | $1.35 lb |
| Eggs | 0.80 doz |
| Sole filets | 0.95 lb |
| Coffee | 1.01 lb |
| Lobsters—whole | 3.50 each |
| Chickens | 0.74 lb |

Calculate the club's *new* potential cost percentage.

3. The following ingredients are required for 80 portions of beef stew. Cost prices and quantities required are also shown. Add 4 percent to total cost for wastage, etc.

| Ingredient | Cost Price | Quantity | |
|------------|-----------|----------|---|
| Boneless beef | $0.90 lb | 35 lbs | 31,5 |
| Flour | 0.06 lb | 2 lbs | .12 |
| Fat | 0.21 lb | 3 lbs | .63 |
| Celery | 0.06 lb | 2 lbs | .12 |
| Carrots | 0.05 lb | 2 lbs | .10 |
| Green peppers | 0.18 lb | 2 lbs | .36 |
| Tomato paste | 1.45 can | 1/2 can | .73 |
| Beef stock | 0.55 gal | 2 gals | 1.10 |
| Potatoes | 0.09 lb | 12 lbs | 1.08 |
| Seasonings | 0.05 total | | .05 |

a. Calculate the cost per portion of this stew. 65¢

b. Assuming that other items to accompany this dish—potato, garnish, side salad—have been costed out at $0.18, what would the selling price have to be to yield a 30 percent food cost? .65 × 3.33 =

c. If the cost of boneless beef goes up by 10 percent, what would the new selling price have to be to maintain a 30 percent food cost?

4. A restaurant serves a 6 oz filet (6 oz before cooking) with baked potato,

vegetable, and side salad. Average weight of filets purchased is 8 1/4 lbs at a cost of $3.40 per pound. Estimated cost of baked potato, vegetable, and side salad is $0.23.

a. How many individual portions can be served from each 8 1/4 lb filet?

b. What would be the cost per portion (including potato, vegetable, and side salad)?

c. What would be the selling price per portion to yield a 60 percent gross profit (gross profit is selling price less food cost)?

5. You have purchased a 40 lb rolled rib roast at $1.65 per pound. Cooking loss is 50 percent.

a. How many 4 oz (cooked weight) portions can be served?

b. What is the cost per portion?

c. What is the cost factor per portion?

d. If the supplier's price goes up to $1.70 per pound, calculate your new cost per portion using the cost factor.

6. You purchase a certain cut of meat in average 43 lb weights. Present cost is $1.35 per pound. It yields the following when butchered:

|  |  |
|---|---|
| Roast | 28 lb |
| Hamburger | 5 lb |
| Stew | 2 lb |
| Bones and waste | 8 lb |

If the hamburger and stew had been purchased separately at market prices, their costs per pound would have been $0.65 and $0.85 per pound, respectively. The roast is subject to 30 percent shrinkage in cooking, and is to be served in 5 oz (cooked weight) portions.

a. Calculate the butchered cost per pound of roast.
b. Calculate the cost per pound of the roast after cooking.
c. Calculate the cost per portion.
d. Calculate the cost factor per pound before cooking, per pound after cooking, and per portion.
e. Using these cost factors, and assuming the supplier's cost to you of the unbutchered cut is decreased from $1.35 to $1.30, recalculate the roast cost per pound before cooking, cost per pound after cooking, and cost per 5 oz cooked weight portion.

7. You have purchased bulk (unbutchered) meat weighing 80 lb at a cost of $1.25 per pound. It yields the following when butchered:

|  |  |
|---|---|
| 30 lb | roast |
| 25 lb | braising meat |
| 15 lb | stewing meat |

| 5 lb | hamburger |
| 5 lb | wastage |

If you had purchased the four usable cuts already butchered from your supplier, he would have charged the following prices:

| Roast | $2.25 lb |
| Braising meat | 1.60 lb |
| Stewing meat | 1.00 lb |
| Hamburger | 0.50 lb |

a. Using the above information, calculate your butchered cost per pound for each of the four cuts.

b. Prove the accuracy of your answer to (a).

c. The 30 lb roast is to be served in 6 oz cooked weight portions, and is subject to a 40 percent weight loss in cooking. How many portions can be served?

d. What is the cost to you per portion?

e. Each portion of roast is served with baked potato, vegetable, salad, and roll and butter. The cost of these other items is calculated to be $0.27. At what price would you sell this entree to yield a 25 percent food cost?

8. You purchase a certain type of bulk (unbutchered) meat at $1 per pound in 45 lb quantities. After butchering, it gives average yields as follows:

| Rump roast | 8 lb |
| Sirloin roast | 14 lb |
| Filet | 3 lb |
| Stewing meat | 9 lb |
| Bones and trim | 11 lb |

If you had purchased the four usable cuts separately (already butchered) from your supplier, he would have charged the following prices:

| Rump roast | $0.80 lb |
| Sirloin roast | 2.50 lb |
| Filet | 3.00 lb |
| Stewing meat | 0.70 lb |

a. Using the above information, calculate your butchered cost per pound for each of the four cuts.

b. Prove the correctness of your answer to (a).

c. Calculate the cost factors for each of the four cuts of meat.

d. Using these cost factors, recalculate your butchered cost per pound for each of the four cuts of meat, assuming the supplier's price of the unbutchered meat goes down from $1 to $0.90.

e. The rump roast is subject to a 35 percent shrinkage loss in cooking. It is served in 4 oz cooked weight portions. At the bulk price of $0.90 per pound, what is your cost of a portion of rump roast?

f. Calculate the cooked weight *portion* cost factor for rump roast.

g. Using this cooked weight portion cost factor, recalculate your portion cost for rump roast if the supplier's price increases from $0.90 to $1.10 for bulk meat.

# 8

# Evaluation of Food Cost Results

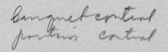

## Objectives

After studying this chapter, the reader will be able to

1. List six possible causes of a difference between a potential cost percentage and the actual cost percentage.

2. Explain the impact that the sales mix has on the calculation of a food cost percentage.

3. Calculate an actual food cost percentage and explain why the sales mix built into this calculation can be the cause of a difference between the actual percentage and the potential percentage based on historical records.

4. Calculate the gross profit of individual menu items or for an entire menu and explain why gross profit can be a more meaningful tool for decision making than a food cost percentage.

5. Calculate a potential food cost percentage based on actual quantities sold of each menu item.

6. Calculate the food cost for each separate sales outlet in a multidepartment operation.

7. Write a two- or three-sentence description of each of the following special procedures: portion control, banquet control, production control.

8. Describe, or draw, each of the forms used in portion control, banquet control, or production control, and complete the forms from given information.

The fifth step in the cycle of control of food production is a periodic evaluation of the results obtained—a comparison of the actual food cost percentage with the potential food cost percentage. Only then can we see how effectively the control system is working.

There will usually be a difference between the two percentages. As long as this difference is small, it can be assumed that no problems exist. The actual result should be within one percentage point of the potential. If the potential is 40 percent, the actual should range between 39 and 41 percent.

If a greater difference exists, it could mean that the potential needs to be recalculated because of rising costs or some other changed circumstances. The cause of the difference could also be one, or a combination, of the following:

Errors in deliveries (poor receiving practices)

Inadequate storeroom controls

Spoilage/wastage in storage or production areas

Failure to follow recipes

Portion sizes not being adhered to

Inventory-taking errors

Excessive cost of employee meals

Pilferage

Increases in purchase costs not adjusted for by changing portion sizes or menu selling prices.

## SALES MIX

Internal problems such as those listed above can be diagnosed and corrected. There is, however, one *external* element over which the restaurant operator has very little control—the quantities of the various menu items customers are going to eat. Different menu items have different markups (and therefore different food cost percentages). As customer preferences change and they eat, on average, more or less of certain menu items, the average food cost percentage will be influenced. The availability of some food items only at certain times of the year, weather, and change of season are some of the factors that can change customer preferences. This changing customer consumption pattern is called the *sales mix*.

When historical records are used to calculate the potential food cost percentage, past information is being used to forecast the future. Since people's eating habits do change from day to day, it is highly unlikely that the actual food cost percentage result for any period will be the same as the precalculated potential food cost percentage. The potential food cost percentage is therefore only an indication of *what we think* the actual food cost will be. To illustrate how potential can differ from actual, see the figures in Table 8.1.

**Table 8.1**

| | Menu Item | *Item* Cost | Sale | Sold | Total Cost | Total Sales | Cost % | Gross Profit |
|---|---|---|---|---|---|---|---|---|
| Potential | 1 | $1.00 | $2.50 | 10 | $10.00 | $ 25.00 | 40.0% | |
| | 2 | 3.00 | 6.00 | 10 | 30.00 | 60.00 | 50.0 | |
| Total | | | | 20 | $40.00 | $ 85.00 | 47.1% | $45.00 |
| Actual | 1 | $1.00 | $2.50 | 5 | $ 5.00 | $ 12.50 | 40.0% | |
| | 2 | 3.00 | 6.00 | 15 | 45.00 | 90.00 | 50.0 | |
| Total | | | | 20 | $50.00 | $102.50 | 48.8% | $52.50 |

The potential food cost percentage is based on the assumption that ten of each item will be sold and is therefore

$$\$\frac{40.00}{85.00} \times 100 = 47.1\%$$

In fact, we sold five of item 1 and fifteen of item 2, and our actual food cost percentage is therefore

$$\$\frac{50.00}{102.50} \times 100 = 48.8\%$$

which is an increase of 1.7 points above what was forecast or expected. A person unfamiliar with the effect a changed sales mix can have on food cost percentages might be concerned about such a difference. Even though the example is an exaggerated one and in practice, with a comprehensive menu over a period of time, sales mix changes would not be as dramatic, the possible effect of a changed sale mix must always be kept in mind when comparing actual food cost with potential food cost.

## GROSS PROFIT

One other important point is illustrated in the examples given above. All other things being equal (labor cost, supplies, expenses, etc.), *it would be better to have a 48.8 percent food cost than a 47.1 percent*. The reason is that we have more *gross profit*, despite a higher food cost percentage. Compare the figures in Table 8.2.

As can be seen, there is $7.50 more available to put in the bank with a 48.8 percent food cost. One must not evaluate only the food cost percentage. A lower food cost percentage, by

Table 8.2

|  | Potential | Actual |
|---|---|---|
| Sales | $ 85.00 | $102.50 |
| Food cost | 40.00 | 50.00 |
| Gross profit | $ 45.00 | $ 52.50 |
| Cost % | 47.1% | 48.8% |

itself, may not be a wise objective. In the long run, the amount of gross profit is much more important. It is for this reason that a restaurant with a 60 percent food cost can be as successful as one with a 20 percent food cost. To improve gross profit, there are a number of alternatives. Purchase costs can be reduced; portion sizes can be made smaller; or selling prices can be increased. But another, and often better, solution is to change what is offered on the menu or to promote those items that yield a greater gross profit. It is generally better, given an equal number of customers, to have each one buy a steak with a $3 gross profit than spaghetti with a $1 gross profit.

Of course, a restaurant selling mainly menu items with a low gross profit cannot suddenly switch to selling only high gross profit items. What is offered on most menus is a combination of both low and high gross profit items, and the selection is generally dictated by the style (decor and atmosphere) of the restaurant, its location, its competition, and the type of customer to which it caters. If a restaurant featuring mostly low gross profit items suddenly changed its menu to high gross profit items, which generally also have higher selling prices, it might find itself losing customers.

## Gross Profit Analysis of Menus

An understanding of gross profit and its effect on net profit offers a useful technique for analyzing alternative menus to determine which is the more profitable, or to determine if the replacement of one item with another on a specific menu is a good idea. For example, consider the following five-item menu:

| Menu Item | Selling Price | Cost Price | Gross Profit | Anticipated Sales | Total Gross Profit |
|-----------|---------------|------------|--------------|-------------------|--------------------|
| 1 | $5.00 | $2.00 | $3.00 | 120 | $ 360.00 |
| 2 | 4.75 | 2.25 | 2.50 | 75 | 187.50 |
| 3 | 6.50 | 2.75 | 3.75 | 40 | 150.00 |
| 4 | 3.95 | 1.45 | 2.50 | 80 | 200.00 |
| 5 | 6.95 | 2.40 | 4.55 | 50 | 227.50 |
| Total | | | | 365 | $1,125.00 |

Gross Profit is arrived at by deducting Cost Price from Selling Price. A method for determining Anticipated Sales is described in the last section of this chapter on production control. Total Gross Profit is a multiplication of Gross Profit (per menu item) ×

Anticipated Sales. The average gross profit per sale for this menu can now be calculated.

$$\frac{\text{Average gross profit}}{\text{per sale}} = \frac{\text{Total gross profit}}{\text{Total anticipated sales}} = \frac{\$1,125.00}{365} = \$3.08$$

(Note that average gross profit per sale cannot be calculated by adding up the five individual gross profit figures and dividing by 5. If we did this ($3.00 + $2.50 + 3.75 + $2.50 + $4.55 = $16.30; $16.30 ÷ 5 = $3.26), we do not get the correct answer, because the individual items have not been "weighted" with the quantities expected to be sold [Anticipated Sales]).

Let us suppose that all five items are changed. The following might be the result:

| Menu Item | Selling Price | Cost Price | Gross Profit | Anticipated Sales | Total Gross Profit |
|-----------|---------------|------------|--------------|-------------------|--------------------|
| 6 | $4.20 | $1.45 | $2.75 | 95 | $  261.25 |
| 7 | 6.15 | 2.70 | 3.45 | 55 | 189.75 |
| 8 | 7.25 | 2.95 | 4.30 | 45 | 193.50 |
| 9 | 3.25 | 1.25 | 2.00 | 100 | 200.00 |
| 10 | 4.50 | 1.80 | 2.70 | 70 | 189.00 |
| Total | | | | 365 | $1,033.50 |

With this particular menu, the average gross profit per sale would be

$$\frac{\$1,033.50}{365} = \$2.83$$

The average gross profit per sale would therefore decline, with this second menu, from $3.08 to $2.83. Management might decide that no menu should produce an average gross profit per sale of less than $3. To increase the second menu's average from $2.83 to $3, we could change one of the menu items. Let us therefore replace menu item 9 with 11:

| Menu Item | Selling Price | Cost Price | Gross Profit | Anticipated Sales | Total Gross Profit |
|-----------|---------------|------------|--------------|-------------------|--------------------|
| Remove 9 | $3.25 | $1.25 | $2.00 | 100 | $200.00 |
| Substitute 11 | 4.05 | 1.35 | 2.70 | 100 | 270.00 |
| Increase | | | | | $ 70.00 |

The new average gross profit per sale would then be

$$\frac{\$1,033.50 + \$70.00}{365} = \frac{\$1,103.50}{365} = \$3.02$$

This change in an individual menu item would permit us to reach our goal.

One assumption built into the preceding illustrations is that by changing an entire menu, or by substituting one menu item for another, there will be no change in anticipated sales. A further assumption is that by changing menus, or menu items, there is no change in other costs (preparation or service labor, operating expenses, etc.). If this were the case, then the Total Gross Profit amount would have to be adjusted accordingly, and the resultant average gross profit per sale would also change.

### Historical Records

As has been demonstrated, historical records of what has been sold of various menu items are a useful starting point in determining a potential food cost percentage. These records will also indicate which menu items could be changed or promoted to influence the overall food cost percentage and gross profit. They are also useful to the chef for forecasting production requirements, even on a daily basis.

When evaluating the actual food cost percentage with a potential calculated from past results, however, the possibility of a changed sales mix must always be kept in mind. For this reason the potential must be updated from time to time, as explained in Chapter 7.


## CALCULATING POTENTIAL FOOD COST
## PERCENTAGE (AN ALTERNATIVE METHOD)

Is there any method of calculating the potential food cost percentage that does not use some previous period's sales mix? The answer is yes. This alternative method is most useful if the menu is relatively limited, but that does not preclude its being used with an extensive menu. It gives a potential food cost percentage that is much more accurate.

For illustrative purposes, let us assume there are only

five items on the menu, with cost and selling prices as shown in Figure 8.1, a sales and potential cost analysis form. At the end of each period (in our case each week), the quantities actually sold of each menu item can be counted up from the sales checks, using a menu item tally sheet (see Figure 8.2). Once these quantities have been calculated, the figures can be inserted on the sales and potential cost analysis form and Total Cost, Total Sales, and the Potential Cost Percentage can be calculated (see Figure 8.4). In our case, it is 38.80 percent. Note that the Total Cost figure of $5,155 is the amount of money we *should have spent* (potential cost) to generate the actual sales we had. It is only a potential cost because we are not sure that all recipes were correctly followed, that there was no excessive wastage, that there was

| | SALES AND POTENTIAL COST ANALYSIS | | | | Week ending | Oct 7 |
|---|---|---|---|---|---|---|
| Item | Item | | Percent Cost | Quantity Sold | Total Cost | Total Sales |
| | Cost | Sale | | | | |
| 1 | 0.75 | 2.00 | 37.5 | | | |
| 2 | 1.25 | 2.75 | 45.5 | | | |
| 3 | 4.00 | 6.50 | 61.5 | | | |
| 4 | 2.10 | 6.00 | 35.0 | | | |
| 5 | 1.50 | 5.50 | 27.3 | | | |

Totals

Potential Cost Percent: Total Cost / Total Sales = ——— x 100 = ———

Actual opening inventory $

Add: purchases for week ———

$

Less: actual closing inventory ———

Actual Cost $———

Actual Cost Percent: Actual Cost / Total Sales = ——— x 100 ———

Difference ———

**Figure 8.1** The sales and potential cost analysis form showing (so far) the Item Cost and Sale prices, and the Percent Cost, of each of the five items we have on our limited menu.

| MENU ITEM TALLY SHEET | | Date _Oct. 7_ | |
|---|---|---|---|
| Item | Sold | | Total |
| 1 | 𝍸𝍸𝍸𝍸𝍸 | | 300 |
| 2 | 𝍸𝍸𝍸𝍸 | | 900 |
| 3 | 𝍸𝍸𝍸𝍸 | | 250 |
| 4 | 𝍸𝍸𝍸𝍸 | 𝍸𝍸 | 1,000 |
| 5 | 𝍸𝍸𝍸𝍸 | | 470 |

**Figure 8.2** The menu item tally sheet summarizes, from sales checks, the quantity of each item sold during the week.

no loss of food, and so on. In order to see if we do have problems of this kind, we can compare our potential cost percentage with the actual cost percentage calculated from inventory and purchases records. In other words, we can compare what the cost should have been (potential) with what it in fact was. This is done by completing the bottom section of the sales and potential cost analysis form (see Figure 8.5). Note that inventory figures include both storeroom and open stock amounts, and that the purchases figure must be adjusted for Transfers In, Transfers Out, and Employee Meals.

The actual cost percentage turns out to be 39.24 percent, which is 0.44 percentage points, or $58 ($5,213 − $5,155), more than we anticipated. A difference must be anticipated because things must be expected to go wrong in the production of food from time to time. As long as the difference is 0.5 percentage points or less it should be considered acceptable. Note that this tolerance amount is only half that which must be permitted using a potential calculated from some past period's sales mix. The reason for the smaller tolerance is that, as mentioned earlier, this alternative method of calculating the potential cost percentage is much more accurate. One thing we can be sure of, using this alternative method, is that *none of the difference was caused by a change in the sales mix*, because we took the actual sales mix

| ITEM | PORTION | | PORTIONS SOLD | | | | | | | TOTAL | TOTAL | |
|---|---|---|---|---|---|---|---|---|---|---|---|---|
| | COST | SALES | | | | | | | TOTAL | COST | COST | SALES |

**SALES AND POTENTIAL COST ANALYSIS**

HOUSE COUNT_____      PERIOD: FROM_____ TO_____

RESTAURANT_____ MENU_____ DATE _____

**Figure 8.3** A form that could be used for sales and potential cost analysis.

that occurred into our calculations. Therefore, if we wish to investigate the cause of the difference, we must check other possibilities (see the list at the beginning of this chapter).

| SALES AND POTENTIAL COST ANALYSIS | | | | Week ending _Oct. 7_ | |
|---|---|---|---|---|---|

| Item | Item Cost | Item Sale | Percent Cost | Quantity Sold | Total Cost | Total Sales |
|---|---|---|---|---|---|---|
| 1 | 0.75 | 2.00 | 37.5 | 300 | $ 225.00 | $ 600.00 |
| 2 | 1.25 | 2.75 | 45.5 | 900 | 1,125.00 | 2,475.00 |
| 3 | 4.00 | 6.50 | 61.5 | 250 | 1,000.00 | 1,625.00 |
| 4 | 2.10 | 6.00 | 35.0 | 1,000 | 2,100.00 | 6,000.00 |
| 5 | 1.50 | 5.50 | 27.3 | 470 | 705.00 | 2,585.00 |
| Totals | | | | | $5,155.00 | $13,285.00 |

Potential Cost Percent: $\dfrac{\text{Total Cost}}{\text{Total Sales}} = \dfrac{5,155.00}{13,285.00}$ x 100 = __38.80 %__

Actual opening inventory                     $

Add: purchases for week                      _____
                                             $

Less: actual closing inventory               _____

Actual Cost                                  $_____

Actual Cost Percent: $\dfrac{\text{Actual Cost}}{\text{Total Sales}} =$ _____ x 100 =   _____

                                             Difference   _____

**Figure 8.4** The form is now completed with Quantity Sold from the tally sheet (see Fig. 8.2), which allows Total Cost, Total Sales, and Potential Cost Percentage to be calculated.

## Potential Cost Percentage Changes

Figure 8.6 shows comparable figures for the following week. Note that, even though there has been no change in menu items, costs, or selling prices, the potential cost percentage has changed from the week ending October 7. It is now 39.28 percent. The reason for this change in the potential is that the *quantities* sold were different this week (the sales mix has changed).

Note also that this week the difference between the potential and actual percentages is 1.50 percentage points, or $171.50 ($4,492.50 − $4,4321.00). In this case, we actually

| SALES AND POTENTIAL COST ANALYSIS | | | | Week ending | Oct. 7 |
|---|---|---|---|---|---|
| Item | Item | | Percentage Cost | Quantity Sold | Total Cost | Total Sales |
| | Cost | Sale | | | | |
| 1 | 0.75 | 2.00 | 37.5 | 300 | $ 225.00 | $ 600.00 |
| 2 | 1.25 | 2.75 | 45.5 | 900 | 1,125.00 | 2,475.00 |
| 3 | 4.00 | 6.50 | 61.5 | 250 | 1,000.00 | 1,625.00 |
| 4 | 2.10 | 6.00 | 35.0 | 1,000 | 2,100.00 | 6,000.00 |
| 5 | 1.50 | 5.50 | 27.3 | 470 | 705.00 | 2,585.00 |
| | | | | | | |
| Totals | | | | | $ 5,155.00 | $13,285.00 |

Potential Cost Percent: $\dfrac{\text{Total Cost}}{\text{Total Sales}} = \dfrac{5,155.00}{13,285.00}$  x  100 =  __38.80%__

Actual opening inventory                    $ 1,743.00

Add: purchases for week                     5,674.00
                                            $7,417.00
Less: actual closing inventory              2,204.00

Actual Cost                                 $ 5,213.00

Actual Cost Percent: $\dfrac{\text{Actual Cost}}{\text{Total Sales}} = \dfrac{5,213.00}{13,285.00}$  x  100 =  __39.24%__

Difference   __0.44__

**Figure 8.5**  The form is finally completed with information from inventory and purchase records, which allows Actual Cost and Actual Cost Percentage to be calculated, and the difference between Potential Cost Percentage and Actual Cost Percentage to be determined.

spent *less* than we expected to produce the food we sold. This could mean that our purchase costs have gone down (an unlikely happening in these inflationary times!), that lower quality food is being purchased at lower prices, that portion sizes are smaller than they should be, and so on. In any event, some corrective action may be necessary.

### Beware of Percentage Changes

One of the dangers of comparing percentages is forgetting that they are only percentages, and not absolute dollars. For example, if food cost in October is 30 percent and in November

| SALES AND POTENTIAL COST ANALYSIS | | | | Week ending | _Oct. 14_ |
|---|---|---|---|---|---|

| Item | Item | | Percent Cost | Quantity Sold | Total Cost | Total Sales |
|---|---|---|---|---|---|---|
| | Cost | Sale | | | | |
| _1_ | _0.75_ | _2.00_ | _37.5_ | _420_ | _$ 315.00_ | _$ 840.00_ |
| _2_ | _1.25_ | _2.75_ | _45.5_ | _630_ | _787.50_ | _1,732.50_ |
| _3_ | _4.00_ | _6.50_ | _61.5_ | _270_ | _1,080.00_ | _1,755.00_ |
| _4_ | _2.10_ | _6.00_ | _35.0_ | _800_ | _1,680.00_ | _4,800.00_ |
| _5_ | _1.50_ | _5.50_ | _27.3_ | _420_ | _630.00_ | _2,310.00_ |

| Totals | | | | | _$4,492.50_ | _$11,437.50_ |

Potential Cost Percent: $\dfrac{\text{Total Cost}}{\text{Total Sales}} = \dfrac{4492.50}{11,437.50}$ x 100 = _39.28 %_

| Actual opening inventory | $ 2,204.00 |
|---|---|
| Add: purchases for week | 4,215.00 |
| | $ 6,419.00 |
| Less: actual closing inventory | 2,098.00 |
| Actual Cost | $ 4,321.00 |

Actual Cost Percent: $\dfrac{\text{Actual Cost}}{\text{Total Sales}} = \dfrac{4321.00}{11,437.50}$ x 100 = _37.78%_

Difference _1.50_

**Figure 8.6** A completed form for the *next* week. Note that both the Actual *and* the Potential Cost Percentages have changed from the preceding period because of a change in the sales mix.

is 33 percent, this is a *10 percent change*, and not just a 3 percent change. The 10 percent is calculated using the following formula:

$$\frac{\text{Amount of change}}{\text{Base period percentage}} \times 100$$

*Percent change*

$$\frac{3}{30} \times 100 = 10\%$$

The reason why it is 10 and not 3 percent can perhaps be more readily understood if we look at some comparative dollar figures:

| | October | November |
|---|---|---|
| Sales | $ 10,000 | $ 10,000 |
| Food cost | $ 3,000 | $ 3,300 |
| Cost % | 30.0 | 33.0 |

The food we purchased in November cost us $300 more than in October for the same amount of sales, and it is obvious that $300 is 10 percent (not 3 percent) more than $3,000. Care must therefore be taken, when comparing percentages, to make sure that a change is converted to real dollar figures.

## Beware of "Averaging" Percentages

A similar danger is inherent in averaging percentages if the wrong method is used. Consider the following information about two menu items:

| Item | Cost | Selling Price | Cost Percentage |
|------|------|---------------|-----------------|
| 1 | $1.00 | $2.50 | 40 |
| 2 | 3.00 | 6.00 | 50 |

The average cost percentage *cannot* be arrived at by adding 40% + 50% = 90% and dividing by 2. The average food cost percentage is influenced by the fact that the items have different costs and selling prices *and* by the fact that different quantities of each will be sold. Reference to Table 8.1 will show that if we sell ten of each item, our average cost percentage will be 47.1; if we sell five of item 1 and fifteen of item 2, our percentage will change to 48.8. It changes upward because item 2 has a 50 percent food cost, and as we sell more of this item, the 50 percent cost factor tends to increase our average. The reverse would occur if we sold more of item 1 than of item 2. The safest method is to divide Total Cost by Total Sales dollars and multiply by 100.

This method can be abbreviated only if an *equal number* of each menu item is sold. This *could* happen, but it would be highly unlikely, particularly if the menu is extensive. In the case of equal quantities sold, there would be no need to multiply menu item costs and sales prices by the quantities to get total cost and total sales. All that is required is to add up the individual item costs, divide by the total of the individual item sales prices, and multiply by 100.

| Item | Cost | Selling Price | Cost Percent |
|------|------|---------------|--------------|
| 1 | $1.00 | $2.50 | 40.0% |
| 2 | 3.00 | 6.00 | 50.0 |
| Average | $4.00 ÷ | $8.50 | X 100 = 47.1% |

## CALCULATING FOOD COST BY SALES AREA

A special problem arises in hotels or food operations in which a number of sales outlets are served from a central kitchen. At each period end, the actual food cost can be determined for the entire operation. For example, suppose we had the following situation at the end of a month:

|  | Banquet Room | Grill Room | Dining Room | Total |
|---|---|---|---|---|
| Sales | $16,000 | $40,000 | $24,000 | $80,000 |
| Food cost |  |  |  | 24,080 |
| Food cost % |  |  |  | 30.1% |

How can we determine the food cost allocation for each of the three sales areas and calculate the food cost percentage for each? The first step is to refer to the appropriate test period potential cost forms (see Figure 7.3) and obtain the potential cost percentage already calculated for the relevant departments. These potential cost percentages are then multiplied by the current period's actual sales for that department, as follows:

| Department | Potential Cost Percentage | X | Actual Sales | Total $ |
|---|---|---|---|---|
| Banquet room | 26.0% | X | $16,000 | $ 4,160 |
| Grill room | 32.0 | X | 40,000 | 12,800 |
| Dining room | 28.0 | X | 24,000 | 6,720 |
| Total potential food cost |  |  |  | $23,680 |

The next step is to calculate a ratio factor between total actual food cost and total potential food cost.

$$\frac{\text{Actual food cost}}{\text{Potential food cost}} = \$ \frac{24,080}{23,680} = 1.0169 \text{ ratio factor}$$

The potential cost percentage by department can now be multiplied by this ratio factor to give an *actual* cost percentage by department, as follows:

*actual cost percentage by dept*

| Department | Potential Cost Percentage | X | Ratio Factor | Actual Cost Percentage |
|---|---|---|---|---|
| Banquet room | 26.0% | X | 1.0169 | 26.44% |
| Grill room | 32.0 | X | 1.0169 | 32.54 |
| Dining room | 28.0 | X | 1.0169 | 28.47 |

Finally, these actual cost percentages can be multiplied by the actual sales to give a food cost by department, as follows:

*food cost by dept*

| Department | Sales | X | Actual Cost Percentage | Food Cost |
|---|---|---|---|---|
| Banquet room | $16,000 | X | 26.44% | $ 4,231 |
| Grill room | 40,000 | X | 32.54 | 13,016 |
| Dining room | 24,000 | X | 28.47 | 6,833 |
| Total | $80,000 | X | 30.1% | $24,080 |

## Multidepartment Establishments

If an establishment has a number of food outlets, the food cost percentages can be calculated for each one. But if we add these percentages together and divide by the number of outlets, we will not get the correct *average* food cost percentage. Assume the following situation:

| Department | Food Cost Percentage |
|---|---|
| A | 30% |
| B | 40 |
| C | 50 |

Now, 30% + 40% + 50% = 120%; 120% ÷ 3 = 40 %. But, except by coincidence or unless each department had exactly the same amount of Total Sales and Total Cost, 40 percent would *not* be our average food cost percentage for the entire operation. We can only calculate that correctly if we combine Total Cost for all three departments, divide by combined Total Sales for all three, and multiply by 100.

*average food cost % for multi dept. est.*

| Department | Total Cost | Total Sales | Food Cost Percentage |
|---|---|---|---|
| A | $ 30,000 | $100,000 | 30% |
| B | 100,000 | 250,000 | 40 |
| C | 150,000 | 300,000 | 50 |
| Average | $280,000 ÷ | $650,000 X | 100 = 43.1% |

## SPECIAL CONTROLS

In addition to the basic food cost percentage control, some special additional controls can be used. Three of these will be discussed: (1) portion control, (2) banquet control, and (3) production control.

### 1. Portion Control

When meat or fish items are purchased in preportioned quantities, even if these items are not controlled in a storeroom situation, it is possible to control their use and sale on a daily basis. Two forms are required: a preportioned food inventory control sheet and a menu item tally sheet.

The inventory sheet is completed daily (see Figure 8.7). The Opening Inventory column is brought forward from the previous day's Closing Inventory column. Figures entered in the Purchased column can be taken from the relevant invoices for that day. The Closing Inventory figure is the actual count of items in the refrigerators or freezers at the end of the day. The figure in

| PRE-PORTIONED FOOD INVENTORY CONTROL SHEET | | | | | | Date _Oct. 1_ | |
|---|---|---|---|---|---|---|---|
| Item | Opening Inventory | Purchased | Closing Inventory | Quantity Used | Quantity Sold | Difference | Explanation |
| Sirloin St. 10 oz | 23 | 24 | 13 | 34 | 32 | -2 | Kitchen Staff |
| " " 8 oz | 11 | 30 | 7 | 34 | 34 | | |
| Filet St. 8 oz | 5 | 36 | 18 | 23 | 23 | | |
| " " 6 oz | 29 | 24 | 14 | 39 | 39 | | |
| Lobster tail | 6 | 12 | 3 | 15 | 14 | -1 | Spoiled |
| | | | | | | | |

**Figure 8.7** This inventory control sheet is used to compare the count of preportioned food items used with the quantity recorded as sold on sales checks.

the Quantity Used column (Opening Inventory + Purchased − Closing Inventory) can then be compared with the Quantity Sold. The Quantity Sold figure is easily calculated by recording the individual sales for each item, taken from the sales checks, on a menu item tally sheet (see Figure 8.8). Any differences between the two figures should be investigated and be explained (see Figure 8.7).

### 2. Banquet Control

A very simple form is all that is required to aid in control of food prepared and served at banquets. The quantities are put into the appropriate places on the form by a person delegated to do this as the waiters carry the food out of the kitchen (see Figure 8.9).

At the end of the function, the banquet manager's or head-waiter's count of the number of guests served by each waiter can be recorded. This should ensure that the waiters or waitresses do not take out of the production area any more dishes of food than they have customers to serve. Such a control form can also be used for customer billing purposes.

### 3. Production Control

To reduce overpurchasing and overproduction, which can lead to wastage, it is advantageous to know each day in advance approximately what quantities to purchase and how much of each

| MENU ITEM TALLY SHEET | | | Date _Oct. 1_ | |
|---|---|---|---|---|
| Item | Sold | | | Total |
| Sirloin Steak  10 oz. | ₦₦ ₦₦ ₦₦ ₦₦ | ₦₦ // | | 32 |
| "         "        8 oz. | ₦₦ ₦₦ ₦₦ ₦₦ | ₦₦ //// | | 34 |
| Filet Steak      8 oz. | ₦₦ ₦₦ ₦₦ ₦₦ | | | 23 |
| "         "        6 oz. | ₦₦ ₦₦ ₦₦ ₦₦ | ₦₦ ₦₦ //// | | 39 |
| Lobster tail | ₦₦ ₦₦ //// | | | 14 |

Figure 8.8 A menu item tally sheet is used to record quantity of each item sold according to the sales checks.

| BANQUET PORTION CONTROL | | | | | | |
|---|---|---|---|---|---|---|
| Room _Ballroom_ | | Function _Constr. Assoc._ | | | Date _Oct. 1_ | |
| Waiter Number | Appetizers | Soups | Salads | Entrees | Desserts | Guests served |
| 1 | 15 | | | 15 | 13 | 15 |
| 2 | 16 | | | 16 | 16 | 16 |
| 3 | 14 | | | 14 | 12 | 14 |
| 4 | 13 | | | 13 | 12 | 13 |
| 5 | | | | | | |
| | | | | | | 18 |
| 30 | 18 | | | 18 | | |
| Totals | 482 | | | 484 | 476 | 484 |

**Figure 8.9** The banquet portion control form is used to compare quantities of items taken from kitchen by servers with count of number of guests actually served.

| DAILY BANQUET COST (FOOD) | | | | | | |
|---|---|---|---|---|---|---|
| Check # | # of Meals Sold | Selling Price | Cost Price | Total Selling | Total Cost | % . |
| | | | | | | |
| | | | | | | |
| | | | | | | |
| | | | | | | |
| | | | | | | |
| | | | | | | |
| | | | | | | |
| | | | | | | |
| | | | | | | |
| | | | | | | |
| | | | | | | |
| | | | | | | |
| | | | | | | |
| | | | | | | |
| | | | | | | |
| | | | | | | |
| TOTALS | | | | $ | $ | % |

**Figure 8.10** A form that could be used for calculation of food cost percentage for each separate banquet.

menu item should be produced. This is relatively easy in a banquet situation, where a known number of customers can be planned on for weeks, or even months, in advance. Even if all those expected do not come, the organization that arranged the banquet is often required to pay for a specified minimum number of guests to protect the hotel or restaurant from overproduction. In the typical restaurant, however, and particularly in those with extensive and constantly changing menus, it becomes much more difficult to plan kitchen production as exactly. One method that lends itself particularly well to operations that have a fixed menu (the various menu items are not changed daily) is quite simple to set up.

The first step is to keep a record, for as long a period as  possible, of the quantity of each of the various menu items sold during this test period. This can best be done on a menu item tally sheet. Figure 8.11 shows such a record for a ten-day period of the entree items sold in a restaurant. The restaurant featured only these five items.

The quantities of each of the items sold can then be converted to a percentage of total items sold. These percentages show the relative popularity of each dish. For example, in the case of Salisbury steak, for each 100 guests served in the restaurant, 20 will eat that menu item (470 ÷ 2,350 x 100 = 20.0%).

| Menu Item | Quantity Sold | Popularity Index |
|---|---|---|
| Salisbury steak | 470 | 20.0% |
| Half chicken | 210 | 8.9 |
| Roast beef | 760 | 32.3 |
| Pork chops | 530 | 22.6 |
| Steak sandwich | 380 | 16.2 |
| Total | 2,350 | 100.0% |

The next step is to forecast each day, for the following day and for each meal period, the anticipated number of customers. This forecast is made by the catering or restaurant manager in consultation with the chef. It will take into consideration any or all of the following factors:

1. Normal number of customers for that meal period and day of the week

2. Any upward or downward trends in this normal number

| MENU ITEM TALLY SHEET | | Period _Oct. 1-10_ |
|---|---|---|
| Item | Sold | Total |
| _Salisbury Steak_ | ⫫⫫ ⫫⫫ ⫫⫫ ⫫⫫ ⫫⫫ | 470 |
| _Half Chicken_ | ⫫⫫ ⫫⫫ ⫫⫫ ⫫⫫⫫ | 210 |
| _Roast Beef_ | ⫫⫫ ⫫⫫ ⫫⫫ ⫫⫫ ⫫ | 760 |
| _Pork Chops_ | ⫫⫫ ⫫⫫ ⫫⫫ ⫫⫫ | 530 |
| _Steak Sandwich_ | ⫫⫫ ⫫⫫ ⫫⫫ ⫫⫫ | 380 |

**Figure 8.11** The menu item tally sheet records, during a test period, the quantity sold of each of the menu items.

3. Any unusual events which are likely to add to or reduce this normal level

4. Expected weather conditions

5. Room occupancy percent (in the case of a restaurant in a hotel)

Once the forecast has been arrived at, the Popularity Index figures can be applied to that forecast to arrive at the anticipated number required for each of the menu items. Let us assume our forecast for the meal period in question is 250 covers. The following will be the forecast for each separate menu item:

| Menu Item | Total Forecast | X | Popularity Index | Anticipated Sales |
|---|---|---|---|---|
| Salisbury steak | 250 | | 20.0% | 50 |
| Half chicken | 250 | | 8.9 | 22 |
| Roast beef | 250 | | 32.3 | 81 |
| Pork chops | 250 | | 22.6 | 57 |
| Steak sandwich | 250 | | 16.2 | 40 |
| Total | | | | 250 |

The final step is to convert the Anticipated Sales into production quantities. This can best be done on a daily food production worksheet (see Figure 8.12). The Anticipated Sales figure is multiplied by the Portion Size to give the Quantity Required. The portion sizes of the various items can be obtained either from the standard portion sizes list (Figure 7.7) or from the related

| DAILY FOOD PRODUCTION WORKSHEET | | | | | Date _Nov. 25_ | | |
|---|---|---|---|---|---|---|---|
| Item | Anticipated Sales | Standard Recipe # | Portion Size (before cooking) | Quantity Required | Quantity Sold | Difference | Reason |
| Salisbury Steak | 50 | 25a | 6 oz. ground round | 19 lb. | 48 | -2 | over-production |
| Half Chicken | 22 | 21 | half fryer | 11 whole | 22 | | ran out 1.15 pm. |
| Roast Beef | 81 | 31c | 6 oz. boneless prime rib | 30 lb. | 75 | -6 | over-production |
| Pork Chops | 57 | 19a | 2 × 5 oz. | 114 chops | 120 | +3 | had extras available |
| Steak Sandwiches | 40 | 42b | 8 oz. sirloin | 20 lb. | 36 | -4 | cooked to order only |
| | | | | | | | |

**Figure 8.12** The daily food production worksheet is used primarily to convert Anticipated Sales into food Quantity Required amounts.

recipe form (Figure 7.6). Copies of this worksheet will be given to the purchaser and to the chef. The purchaser can use the information to aid in buying to meet the anticipated sales. Overpurchasing can thus be reduced.

At the end of each meal period, the Quantity Sold figures can be entered (taken from sales checks), the difference between Anticipated Sales and Quantity Sold can be calculated, and the reason for this difference can be recorded. Any necessary corrective action can then be taken by the food and beverage manager and/or the chef.

Although the daily food production worksheet shown illustrates only the main ingredient for each of the entree items, it could be expanded to include quantities required for accompanying items such as potatoes, vegetables, and salads. Similar worksheets could also be prepared for each day and meal period for soups, appetizers and desserts.

## SUMMARY

One of the most important steps in the control cycle is a periodic evaluation of the results. In other words, a comparison must be made between the actual food cost achieved and the potential (expected) food cost. How close did we come to our objective?

Even with tight control over the food storeroom, standard recipes in effect and being followed, and good control over food "leakage," there is one factor over which management can exercise little control: sales mix.

A change in customer menu preferences, because each menu item offered may have a different cost percentage, can mean quite a change in the overall food cost percentage. Establishments that use historical sales mix figures to forecast or calculate the potential food cost percentage are using imperfect information about the future. Sales mix is bound to change, not only on a day-to-day basis, but also by season.

One way to discount an unknown sales mix is to calculate the potential cost *after* the event, using the actual sales mix that occurred during the period under review. The sales checks listing items actually sold can be used. Number Sold X Item Cost (for each separate menu item) will give a Total Cost. Number Sold X Item Selling Price (for each separate menu item) will give Total Sales. Total Cost divided by Total Sales and multiplied by 100 gives a potential cost percentage. Potential cost percentage can then be compared with actual cost percentage. (The Actual Cost is calculated from inventory and purchase records. Actual Cost divided by Total Sales and multiplied by 100 gives us the actual cost percentage.)

The two results should be no more than half of one percentage point apart. If the difference is greater, further checking may be required. A change in the sales mix, however, will *not* be the reason for any of the difference. The reason will probably be found among the items on pages 137-138.

Because the sales mix will change each period, the potential cost percentage will change, along with the actual cost percentage. But the two should change in tandem.

A lowering of the potential and actual cost percentages is not necessarily a good objective. When analyzing results, the gross profit resulting from a certain mix of sales must always be kept in mind. A high cost percentage with a high gross profit is better than a low cost percentage and a low gross profit, all other variables being equal.

When a number of sales outlets are served from a central kitchen, the food cost for the entire operation can be calculated at the end of each period, but some additional arithmetic is necessary if a food cost and a food cost percentage are desired for separate sales area.

Finally, food production control can be supplemented by special controls in certain situations. Three were discussed: portion control (a comparison of preportioned items used according to inventory records is made, each day, with the count of the same items sold according to the sales checks); banquet control (a record of the number of items taken out of the kitchen by each waiter or waitress is compared with the count, made by the banquet manager, of the number of guests served by each waiter or waitress); and production control (a method that attempts to match purchase and production quantities of each separate menu item to anticipated sales of that item).

## DISCUSSION QUESTIONS

1. What are some of the possible causes of a difference between the potential food cost percentage and the actual food cost percentage?

2. Why is a potential food cost percentage based on historical records not necessarily indicative of what the *actual* food cost percentage will be?

3. If you have a choice between selling a menu item with a 30 percent food cost and one with a 50 percent food cost, why is it not necessarily best to sell the one with the lowest food cost percentage?

4. What is a menu item tally sheet? *record of sales of each menu item. [handwritten]*

5. In establishments where it is possible to calculate the potential food cost percentage *after* the period is over, why will this potential probably change every period? *availing food items at certain time of year [handwritten]*

6. Describe briefly how portion control can be implemented.

7. Why does the quantity of what we sell of various menu items have any influence on the overall food cost percentage?

## MULTIPLE CHOICE/DISCUSSION QUESTIONS

1. The fact that restaurant A has sales of $120,000 and a food cost of 40 percent, while restaurant B has sales (for the same period) of $100,000 and a food cost of 30 percent means

   a. Restaurant A's food cost is too high.

b. Something is wrong in restaurant B because its food cost is too low.

c. Restaurant B has a better control system.

d. Restaurant A should change its sales mix.

e. None of the above is necessarily true.

2. The main purpose of setting a potential food cost percentage is to

a. Know in advance what your food cost is going to be.

b. Be able to calculate a food cost percentage each day.

c. Have a figure against which actual food cost can be compared.

d. Be able to figure out in advance what the gross profit is going to be.

e. Keep actual food cost up to date with changing purchase cost of foods.

3. If the actual food cost percentage is lower than the potential food cost percentage we can be sure that

a. The control system is working perfectly.

b. The potential was set too high.

c. The accounting control office is smarter than the food and beverage department.

d. Our sales mix has improved.

e. All of the above are true.

f. None of the above is necessarily correct.

## PROBLEMS    *anticipated sales*

1. The Rusty Rail Restaurant features only three entree items on its menu and on the average anticipates selling 50 of each item each day. Cost and selling prices and food cost percentage are as follows:

| Item | Cost | Selling Price | | Food Cost % | | |
|------|------|---------------|---|-------------|---|---|
| 1 | $2.20 | $4.40 | *5°* | 50.0 | *110* | *220* |
| 2 | 1.80 | 4.50 | *5°* | 40.0 | *72* | *180* |
| 3 | 1.00 | 3.30 | *5°* | 30.0 | *30.* | *99* |

a. What will its potential food cost percentage be?    *$2.5    42    499*

b. If it actually sells, on average, 100 of item 1 and only 25 each of items 2 and 3, is its actual food cost percentage going to be higher or lower than its projected potential, and *why?*

2. The Delightful Dining Room, during the week of November 1 to 7, had the following items on its menu, with cost and selling prices, and quantity sold during that week, as shown:

| Item | Cost | Selling Price | Quantity Sold |
|---|---|---|---|
| Lobster | $3.00 | $7.50 | 100 |
| Steak | 2.50 | 5.50 | 200 |
| Salmon | 1.50 | 3.00 | 650 |
| Roast beef | 1.80 | 4.00 | 50 |

a. Calculate, for each of the four items, the menu item cost percentage.

b. Calculate the overall potential food cost percentage for that week.

3. A company cafeteria had food sales in January of $1,000, and a food cost of $400. The following month, sales increased 20 percent and food cost was $528. By how many percentage points has the food cost percentage increased from January to February?

4. A hotel has three departments with the following food sales and cost percentages. What is its average food cost percentage for the entire operation?

| Department | Sales | Cost % |
|---|---|---|
| Banquet | $ 40,000 | 35.0 |
| Dining room | 120,000 | 30.0 |
| Coffee shop | 30,000 | 40.0 |

5. You have the following information about two alternative menus:

| | Menu A | | | | Menu B | |
|---|---|---|---|---|---|---|
| Item | Selling Price | Cost Price | | Item | Selling Price | Cost Price |
| 1 | $6.00 | $2.60 | 3.46 | 5 | $4.95 | $2.25 | 2.70 |
| 2 | 3.50 | 1.50 | 2.00 | 6 | 3.80 | 1.95 | 1.85 |
| 3 | 4.75 | 1.65 | 3.10 | 7 | 5.50 | 2.10 | 3.40 |
| 4 | 5.25 | 2.30 | 2.95 | 8 | 5.25 | 1.75 | 3.50 |

*(handwritten totals: 6.10; 2.00; 4.00)*

On a particular day anticipated sales are 310, broken down as follows for each of the two menus:

| | Menu A | | Menu B |
|---|---|---|---|
| Item | Anticipated Sales | Item | Anticipated Sales |
| 1 | 75 | 5 | 60 |
| 2 | 120 | 6 | 135 |
| 3 | 65 | 7 | 70 |
| 4 | 50 | 8 | 45 |

a. In terms of gross profit, which menu would be more profitable?

b. On menu B, Item 9 is substituted for Item 8. Item 9 has a selling price of $6 and a cost price of $2. If the substitution took place, with no change in anticipated sales, would your answer to (a) change?

6. The Dandy Dining Room during October had an actual food cost of $10,154.69. During this same month, its food sales were $31,114.75.
   a. Calculate its actual food cost percentage.
   b. Compare this with its potential food cost percentage calculated in Problem 1, Chapter 7.
   c. What possible reasons are there for the difference between the two results?

7. The sales records for a dining room with a menu limited to six items show the following quantities sold during December. Item cost and selling prices are also indicated.

| Item | Cost | Selling Price | Quantity Sold |
|------|------|---------------|---------------|
| 1 | $1.75 | $5.00 | 2,000 |
| 2 | 2.25 | 7.00 | 2,200 |
| 3 | 1.10 | 4.50 | 4,400 |
| 4 | 2.00 | 6.00 | 1,300 |
| 5 | 2.25 | 5.00 | 600 |
| 6 | 2.00 | 8.00 | 500 |

Inventory and purchase records provide the following further information for the same month:

Actual opening inventory   $ 8,284
Purchases                  17,779
Actual closing inventory   7,716
*Calculate*
a. The potential cost percentage for each of the six menu items.
b. The overall potential food cost percentage.
c. The actual food cost percentage. Would the difference between the two percentages be acceptable?  *Actual cost*
d. The inventory turnover rate.  *Total Sale*

8. The City Hotel's test period potential cost percentage figures are as follows:
   Banquet room   26%
   Grill room     35%
   Snack bar      27%

In March the actual sales by department and total food cost for all three departments combined are

| Department | Sales | Combined Food Cost |
|------------|-------|--------------------|
| Banquet room | $15,420 | |
| Grill room | 32,917 | $20,351 |
| Snack bar | 19,108 | |

*Calculate*

a. The overall actual food cost percentage.

b. The actual food cost percentage and food cost dollars, by department.

9. A test period indicated the following quantities of menu items were sold in a restaurant during the lunch period:

| Menu Item | Sold |
|:---:|:---:|
| 1 | 322 |
| 2 | 849 |
| 3 | 617 |
| 4 | 430 |
| 5 | 476 |
| 6 | 398 |
| 7 | 517 |

On March 6 the restaurant manager and the chef forecast that 420 total covers would be sold at lunch on March 7.

a. Calculate the popularity index for each of the seven menu items.

b. Calculate for March 7, the anticipated sales for each of the menu items.

c. If the recipe for menu item 1 calls for 6 oz of roast beef, before cooking, calculate the total quantity of roast beef required for production on March 7.

# 9

# Beverage Cost Control: The Storeroom

## Objectives

After studying this chapter, the reader will be able to

1. Identify the two major procedures for verifying the accuracy of beverage deliveries.
2. Explain why it is best to separate the recording of beverage purchase cost and sale dollars into the three separate categories of liquor, beer, and wine.
3. Explain the use of perpetual inventory cards and requisitions in beverage control.
4. Complete a perpetual inventory card or requisition for beverages from given information.
5. Explain the value of a "par stock" system and an "empty bottle return" system of beverage control.
6. Describe and carry out calculations using the first-in/first-out method of beverage storeroom inventory control.
7. Complete and balance a daily liquor receiving and issues report.
8. Calculate beverage cost percentages and beverage inventory turnovers.

The use of the word "beverage" in this chapter is intended to cover all types of alcoholic beverages. As is the case in food cost control, beverage cost control begins with the ordering and purchasing process.

## ORDERING/PURCHASING

The same person who does the food ordering and purchasing can also handle the purchasing of alcoholic beverages. Each day, the beverage room storekeeper can provide this person with a list of items required to bring the beverage stock up to par. If any special quantities of liquor are required for a banquet function, then the banquet manager or some other person responsible must make the requirements known to the purchaser.

The record of items ordered can be handled by means of an order form or order book similar to the one used for food (see Figure 3.8).

### Receiving

The receiver must check that (a) the quantities received agree with the quantities recorded on the invoice accompanying the shipment, and (b) the quantities received, and the prices on the invoice, agree with the same information recorded on the order form. Once these facts have been confirmed, the receiver can stamp the invoice and initial it in the appropriate places, using the same rubber stamp used on food invoices (see Chapter 4).

## Daily Liquor Receiving and Issues Report

At the end of each day, the receiver will complete a daily liquor receiving and issues report (see Figure 9.1), filling in information from invoices in the relevant columns. Each day's column total is added to the balance brought forward from the preceding day's report. In this way an accumulated (to date) cost figure can be obtained for each category of purchase during the period. It is usual for beverages to be divided into three categories: liquor, beer, and wine. The reason for this is that each of these three categories will generally have a widely different markup. A change in the sales mix among the three from one period to the next can have an effect on the overall cost percentage, and the cause for this change in the sales mix could be buried if cost and sales figures were not kept separate. Consider the following illustration:

| Item | Last Month | | | This Month | | |
|------|------|------|------|------|------|------|
|      | Cost | Sales | Cost % | Cost | Sales | Cost % |
| Liquor | $ 6,090 | $21,000 | 29.0% | $ 6,300 | $21,000 | 30.0% |
| Beer | 1,170 | 3,000 | 39.0 | 2,400 | 6,000 | 40.0 |
| Wine | 5,880 | 12,000 | 49.0 | 1,500 | 3,000 | 50.0 |
| Total | $13,140 | $36,000 | | $10,200 | $30,000 | |
| Overall cost % | $\frac{\$13,140}{\$36,000} \times 100 = 36.5$ | | | $\frac{\$10,200}{\$30,000} \times 100 = 34.0$ | | |

Note that the overall cost has declined this month from 36.5 to 34 percent. Normally this would be indicative, assuming no change in basic purchase costs and selling prices of drinks, of greater efficiency by the bartenders. But, in fact, the individual category cost percentages have all *increased*. (Note, for example, that liquor cost percentage has increased from 29 to 30 percent; the other two have increased similarly). In other words, costs have *climbed* relative to sales. The cause of the decline of the overall cost percentage is due *entirely* to a change in the sales mix (in proportion to total sales, more liquor has been sold this month

| DAILY LIQUOR RECEIVING AND ISSUES REPORT | | Date _Nov. 7_ | | |
|---|---|---|---|---|
| RECEIVING | | | | |
| Supplier | Invoice Total | Liquor | Beer | Wine |
| _Stevens & Co._ | _431. 05_ | _431.05_ | | |
| _Wine Imports_ | _117.21_ | | | _117.21_ |
| | | | | |
| | | | | |
| | | | | |
| Today's purchases | _548.26_ | _431.05_ | | _117.21_ |
| Previous balance forward | _1201.94_ | _404.05_ | _319.20_ | _478.69_ |
| Total purchases to date | _1750.20_ | _835.10_ | _319.20_ | _595.90_ |
| ISSUES | | | | |
| Bar or department | Total Requisitions | Liquor | Beer | Wine |
| | | | | |
| | | | | |
| | | | | |
| Today's requisitions | | | | |
| Previous balance forward | | | | |
| Total requisitions to date | | | | |
| STORE-ROOM RECONCILIATION | | | | |
| | Total | Liquor | Beer | Wine |
| Opening inventory | | | | |
| Add: purchases to date | | | | |
| Less: requisitions to date | | | | |
| Equals: closing inventory | | | | |
| Actual closing inventory | | | | |
| Difference | | | | |
| Explanation | | | | |

**Figure 9.1** The daily liquor receiving and issues report showing purchases made on this day, and accumulated purchases for the week ending November 7.

than beer or wine). This being the case, if the individual category cost percentages had been kept as they were last month, our overall cost percentage should have been *less than 34 percent!* This only becomes apparent by separating costs and sales by category.

## STOREROOM CONTROL

*All* liquor, beer, and wine purchases should be put into a central beverage storeroom before being issued to the bar(s). The beverage storeroom is best located separate from the food storeroom and as close to the main bar as possible to reduce distances when bottles are moved from the storeroom to the bar. The food storeroom storekeeper may be made responsible for the beverage storeroom. In a large hotel, a separate full-time beverage storekeeper may be needed. In either case, only one designated employee should be in charge of this area. None of the bar staff should have access to this storage room.

### Perpetual Inventory Cards

Perpetual inventory cards should be maintained for each separate brand or type carried in stock (see Chapter 5 for a discussion of perpetual inventory cards). Generally the storekeeper is responsible for keeping these cards up to date. However, if it is decided that the cards should be kept in the control office, then the storekeeper could be supplied with bin cards (see Figure 5.4).

### Par stock

For each item or type of liquor, beer, or wine, management should prepare a par stock list to be posted in the bar(s). The par stock is the quantity of each item that should be on hand prior to each day's business. These par stock levels can be adjusted up or down by management when necessary (change in customer preferences, seasonal changes, and so on). The control staff should spot-check the bar(s) from time to time to ensure that these par stock levels are being adhered to.

### Requisitions

Requisitions (see Chapter 5) will be completed each day by the bartender on duty in order to bring the stock in the bar up to the par level. A system of full bottle replacement is recommended. Under this system, issues to the bar, authorized by requisition, should be made only if the requisition is accompanied by empty bottles of the same quantity and type listed on the requisition. Some establishments identify full bottles of liquor

**Figure 9.2** Control of the beverage storeroom, as is the case with the food storeroom, can be accomplished by using perpetual inventory cards and requisitions.

issued with difficult-to-duplicate coding devices (in some cases a different code for each separate bar) to ensure that the empty bottles returned are authentic. These empty bottles must be destroyed immediately by the storekeeper. The control office should spot-check the bar(s) from time to time to see that no "unauthorized" (uncoded) bottles are being used.

Once the bottles have been issued, the storekeeper will cost out the requisitions by copying the costs from the appropriate perpetual inventory cards. In liquor, beer, and wine costing, it is suggested that, for accuracy, the first-in/first-out method be used. In other words, where purchase prices of items are changing, a note should be made on the perpetual inventory card of the quantity on hand at each separate price. The earliest (first) bottles purchased at a specific price will be the first ones issued and the first ones costed out on requisitions.

To illustrate, suppose we had five bottles of a certain item on hand at a cost of $5 each. Two dozen more were purchased at a price of $5.25 each. Figure 9.3 shows the perpetual inventory card. If a requisition is received from the bartender for eight bottles to be issued, the requisition would be costed out as follows:

$$5 \text{ bottles @ } \$5.00 = \$25.00$$
$$3 \text{ bottles @ } \$5.25 = \underline{\phantom{0}15.75}$$
$$\$40.75$$

The perpetual inventory card would then show twenty-one bottles still in stock at $5.25 each.

When all requisitions have been costed out for that day, the total costs can be inserted on the liquor receiving and issue report in the Issues section in the appropriate columns (see Figure 9.4). Note that the requisition totals, by category, are accumulated with balances brought forward from the preceding day's report. (For example, with reference to Figure 9.4, in the Liquor column of the Issues section, the figure of $697.90 on the Previous Balance Forward line would have been the Total Requisitions To Date figure in the liquor column of the report of November 6).

## STOREROOM INVENTORY

Inventory should be taken of storeroom items once a week. Inventory sheets (or an inventory book) similar in design to those illustrated in Chapter 5 can be used. Items on the shelves should be located in the same order as they are on the inventory sheet, and the perpetual inventory cards should be kept in corresponding order.

| Date | In | Out | Balance |
|------|-----|-----|---------|
| forward | | | 5 |
| Nov. 7 | 24 | | 29 (5 c @ 5.00 / 24 c @ 5.25) |
| | | | |
| | | | |

**Figure 9.3**

| DAILY LIQUOR RECEIVING AND ISSUES REPORT | | | Date _Nov. 7_ | |
|---|---|---|---|---|
| RECEIVING | | | | |
| Supplier | Invoice Total | Liquor | Beer | Wine |
| Stevens & Co. | 431.05 | 431.05 | | |
| Wine Imports | 117.21 | | | 117.21 |
| | | | | |
| | | | | |
| | | | | |
| Today's purchases | 548.26 | 431.05 | | 117.21 |
| Previous balance forward | 1201.94 | 404.05 | 319.20 | 478.69 |
| Total purchases to date | 1750.20 | 835.10 | 319.20 | 595.90 |
| ISSUES | | | | |
| Bar or department | Total Requisitions | Liquor | Beer | Wine |
| Main Bar | 215.08 | 126.14 | 20.80 | 68.14 |
| Banquet | 105.40 | 105.40 | | |
| | | | | |
| Today's requisitions | 320.48 | 231.54 | 20.80 | 68.14 |
| Previous balance forward | 1060.79 | 697.90 | 42.30 | 320.59 |
| Total requisitions to date | 1381.27 | 929.44 | 63.10 | 388.73 |
| STORE-ROOM RECONCILIATION | | | | |
| | Total | Liquor | Beer | Wine |
| Opening inventory | | | | |
| Add: purchases to date | | | | |
| Less: requisitions to date | | | | |
| Equals: closing inventory | | | | |
| Actual closing inventory | | | | |
| Difference | | | | |
| Explanation | | | | |

**Figure 9.4** At the end of each day the Issues section of the report can be completed from information taken from requisitions for that day.

One person should check the count of items on the shelves while the other verifies this figure against the card and then records it on the inventory sheet. Differences between count and card should be traced back by reference to the related invoices and/or requisitions. If differences cannot be accounted for, the

| BEVERAGE REQUISITION | | | | | | | | | | **2951** | |
|---|---|---|---|---|---|---|---|---|---|---|---|

NAME OF BAR_____ DATE _____

| BIN NO. | N A M E | ON HAND | ORDERED | ISSUED | | | | | UNIT COST | TOTAL COST | |
|---|---|---|---|---|---|---|---|---|---|---|---|
| | | | | GAL. | QTS. | 5TH | PTS. | SPL | | | |
| | | | | | | | | | | | |
| | | | | | | | | | | | |
| | | | | | | | | | | | |
| | | | | | | | | | | | |
| | | | | | | | | | | | |
| | | | | | | | | | | | |
| | | | | | | | | | | | |
| | | | | | | | | | | | |
| | | | | | | | | | | | |
| | | | | | | | | | | | |
| | | | | | | | | | | | |
| | | | | | | | | | | | |
| | | | | | | | | | | | |
| | | | | | | | | | | | |
| | | | | | | | | | | | |
| | | | | | | | | | | | |
| | | | | | | | | | | | |
| | | | | | | | | | | | |
| | | | | | | | | | | | |
| | | | | | | | | | | | |
| | | | | | | | | | | | |
| | | | | | | | | | | | |
| | | | | | | | | | | | |
| | | | | | | | | | | | |
| | | | | | | | | | | | |
| | | | | | | | | | | | |
| | | | | | | | | | | | |

Ordered By:_____ Filled BY:_____ Received BY: _____

Approved BY: _____

Figure 9.5 A typical beverage requisition used in industry.

card Balance figure must be corrected to show the actual count of items on hand. If differences are numerous or large, more intensive investigation may be required to determine the cause of the leakage.

| | | | | | | |
|---|---|---|---|---|---|---|
| | | INTER-BAR  TRANSFERS | | | N⁰  2552 | |
| | | | | | | |

FROM_____ BAR

TO_____ BAR                DATE_____

| BIN NO. | N A M E | SIZE | QUANTITY | UNIT COST | TOTAL COST | |
|---|---|---|---|---|---|---|
| | | | | | | |
| | | | | | | |
| | | | | | | |
| | | | | | | |
| | | | | | | |
| | | | | | | |
| | | | | | | |
| | | | | | | |
| | | | | | | |
| | | | | | | |
| | | | | | | |
| | | | | | | |
| | | | | | | |
| | | | | | | |
| | | | | | | |
| | | | | | | |
| | | | | | | |
| | | | | | | |
| | | | | | | |
| | | | | | | |
| | | | | | | |
| | | | | | | |
| | | | | | | |
| | | | | | | |
| | | | | | | |
| | | | | | | |
| | | | | | | |
| | | | | | | |
| | | | | | | |

ORDERED BY_____ FILLED BY _____

**Figure 9.6**  Sample of a form that could be used for interbar transfers in establishments which have more than one bar.

## Reconciliation of Actual Inventory with Liquor Receiving and Issues Report

At the end of each period (in our case a week), a reconciliation can be made between the liquor receiving and issues report and the actual inventory of liquor, beer, and wine in the storeroom. Refer to the bottom section of the report (Figure 9.7). The Opening Inventory figures would be the *actual* inventory values at the end of the previous period. The Purchases To Date figures are copied from the top section of the report. The Requisitions To Date figures are copied from the center section of the report. As long as quantities and costs have been properly recorded on the perpetual inventory cards and on the requisitions during the period, the following equation will give us a Closing Inventory figure:

Opening inventory

+

Purchases to date

−

Requisitions to date

=

Closing inventory

This closing inventory figure should agree with an actual inventory value according to the inventory sheets. Major differences should be investigated and explained. Minor differences may occur from rounding out bottle costs on the perpetual inventory cards to the nearest cent. When the two inventory figures are in agreement, it can be assumed that the storeroom is adequately controlled. The other area requiring control is the bar itself. This will be discussed in Chapter 10.

### Inventory Turnover     ½ to 1 time / month

Food inventory turnover was discussed in Chapter 5. The typical food turnover is usually between two to four times a month. Beverage inventory turnover is generally from half to one time a month. It is calculated using the same general equation as that used for food:

$$\text{Beverage inventory turnover} = \frac{\text{Beverage cost for the month}}{\text{Average beverage inventory}}$$

Reference to the section on inventory turnover in Chapter 5 will show how cost for the month and average inventory are calculated. This average inventory figure is (as is the case with food) made up of both the storeroom inventory *and* the production inventory.

| DAILY LIQUOR RECEIVING AND ISSUES REPORT | | | Date _Nov. 7_ | |
|---|---|---|---|---|
| RECEIVING | | | | |
| Supplier | Invoice Total | Liquor | Beer | Wine |
| _Stevens & Co._ | _431.05_ | _431.05_ | | |
| _Wine Imports_ | _117.21_ | | | _117.21_ |
| | | | | |
| | | | | |
| | | | | |
| Today's purchases | _548.26_ | _431.05_ | | _117.21_ |
| Previous balance forward | _1201.94_ | _404.05_ | _319.20_ | _478.69_ |
| Total purchases to date | _1750.20_ | _835.10_ | _319.20_ | _595.90_ |
| ISSUES | | | | |
| Bar or department | Total Requisitions | Liquor | Beer | Wine |
| _Main Bar_ | _215.08_ | _126.14_ | _20.80_ | _68.14_ |
| _Banquet_ | _105.40_ | _105.40_ | | |
| | | | | |
| Today's requisitions | _320.48_ | _231.54_ | _20.80_ | _68.14_ |
| Previous balance forward | _1060.79_ | _697.90_ | _42.30_ | _320.59_ |
| Total requisitions to date | _1381.27_ | _929.44_ | _63.10_ | _388.73_ |
| STORE-ROOM RECONCILIATION | | | | |
| | Total | Liquor | Beer | Wine |
| Opening inventory | _3071.06_ | _2042.19_ | _215.10_ | _813.77_ |
| Add: purchases to date | _1750.20_ | _835.10_ | _319.20_ | _595.90_ |
| Less: requisitions to date | _1381.27_ | _929.44_ | _63.10_ | _388.73_ |
| Equals: closing inventory | _3439.99_ | _1947.85_ | _471.20_ | _1020.94_ |
| Actual closing inventory | _3434.76_ | _1942.70_ | _471.20_ | _1020.86_ |
| Difference | _5.23_ | _5.15_ | _0_ | _0.08_ |
| Explanation | | _1 bottle gin broken_ | | |
| | | | | |

**Figure 9.7** At the end of each period (in this case a week), a Storeroom Reconciliation can be made by completing the bottom section of the report. Major differences should be explained.

In other words, to the storeroom inventory value (discussed in this chapter) we must add the value of the beverages at the bar to obtain a total inventory.

## SUMMARY

Control of beverages is required at two main points: the storeroom
and the bar. This chapter covered storeroom control. *All* beverages
should be put into the storeroom before being issued to the bar.

Control begins with the ordering and purchasing process,
which is similar to that used for food (see Chapter 3). As beverages
are received, they should be checked by the receiver to ensure that
the quantities agree with the accompanying invoice, and that the
quantities and prices on the invoice agree with what was ordered.

The basic control form for the storeroom is a daily liquor
receiving and issues report. Each day, invoice information about
what has been received can be recorded on the Receiving section
of this report. Note that costs are segregated on this report into
three major categories: liquor, beer, and wine. The reason these
cost (and also the sales) figures are kept separate is that each of
these three categories has a different markup in most cases; if
costs and sales are not kept separate, a distorted overall beverage
cost percentage might result. Each separate item of beverage put
into the storeroom will be recorded on a perpetual inventory
card. The invoices provide the information recorded on the cards
concerning quantities coming in and their costs.

Each day, the bartender must fill in a requisition to obtain
beverages from the storeroom to bring his bar stock up to par, and
also turn in empty bottles (which must be subsequently destroyed
by the storekeeper) for full ones. The storekeeper deducts quantities issued from the perpetual inventory cards. The quantity on
hand in the storeroom should thus always agree with the Balance
figure on the card. At the same time, he copies cost information
from the card onto the requisition. At the end of each day,
the requisition(s) can be totaled and the information recorded in
the Issues section of the daily liquor receiving and issues report.

At the end of each period, the bottom section of this
report can be used to make an inventory reconciliation. This
reconciliation will indicate whether or not what should be in the
storeroom is actually there. Differences should be investigated.

Inventory turnover in a beverage department is usually
between half to one time a month. Remember that the inventory

figure for this calculation is made up of both the inventory in the storeroom and the inventory at the bar itself.

## DISCUSSION QUESTIONS

1. What items should be checked when alcoholic beverages are received?

2. Why, on the daily liquor receiving and issues report, should purchases be broken down into liquor, beer and wine?

3. Describe briefly how perpetual inventory cards and requisitions are used in storeroom beverage control.

4. Why should empty liquor bottles be returned to the beverage storekeeper by the bartender(s)?

5. Describe how the first-in/first-out method of pricing items in the beverage storeroom works.

6. Define "beverage inventory turnover"; what is the normal turnover rate per month?

## MULTIPLE CHOICE/DISCUSSION QUESTIONS

1. A par stock list should be posted in the bar so that
    a. Management can be sure that customers will be given a choice of brands.
    b. Inventory taking at month-end will be made easier for the control staff.
    c. The bartender each day will know how many bottles of each type or brand to order from the storeroom to replenish the bar.
    d. No unauthorized bottles of liquor can possibly be used at the bar.
    e. The control office can quickly identify that all bottles are properly coded.

2. The daily liquor receiving and issues report is used primarily
    a. To calculate a daily liquor cost percentage.
    b. To give full details about all purchases of beverages.
    c. To charge the appropriate bars with cost of items requisitioned from the beverage storeroom.

  d. To summarize inventory turnover rates.
  e. To aid in beverage storeroom inventory control.

3. If a bar sold only liquor and beer and liquor had a *higher markup* than beer, and in July the liquor *cost percentage* increased while that of beer stayed the same, and there was absolutely *no change* from June to July in sales dollars either by category or in total, we could expect (Note: gross profit is sales minus cost)

  a. The overall beverage cost percentage to have declined from June to July.
  b. The gross profit to have declined from June to July.
  c. The gross profit to have increased from June to July.
  d. The overall beverage cost percentage *and* the gross profit to have increased from June to July.
  e. The overall beverage cost percentage *and* the gross profit to have decreased from June to July.

## PROBLEMS

1. The Swizzle Stick Bar uses the first-in/first-out method of issuing liquor from the beverage storeroom to the bar. On December 4 it had on hand three bottles of a particular brand of Scotch at $6.15 each. On that date, two dozen more bottles were purchased and received at a price of $75.60 a case (twelve bottles to a case). On December 5 the bar manager submitted a requisition for eight bottles of this brand of Scotch to be delivered from the storeroom to the bar. What total cost will appear on the requisition for this transaction?

2. A hotel's cocktail lounge has the following sales and beverage cost percentage results for two successive months:

| | January | | February | |
| Item | Sales | Cost % | Sales | Cost % |
| --- | --- | --- | --- | --- |
| Liquor | $24,321 | 30% | $25,840 | 29% |
| Beer | 5,107 | 45 | 6,405 | 50 |
| Wine | 4,211 | 60 | 4,104 | 65 |

  a. Calculate, for each month, the overall beverage cost percentage.
  b. Comment on the results insofar as any changes have occurred from January to February.
  c. Calculate the gross profit for each month, and comment.

3. The daily liquor receiving and issues report for the Bamboo Bar for the period March 1 to 6 shows the following:

|  | Liquor | Beer | Wine |
|---|---|---|---|
| Purchases to date | $508.40 | $206.18 | $174.96 |
| Requisitions to date | 431.14 | 180.06 | 352.04 |

On March 7 the following two purchases were made: Liquor Wholesalers Ltd., $179.68 (of which $164.28 was liquor and the balance beer), and Wine Importing Co., $152.07 (all wine). Two requisitions were processed on March 7:

|  | Liquor | Beer | Wine |
|---|---|---|---|
| Bar  A | $ 87.20 | $ 41.16 | $ 75.97 |
| Bar  B | 61.07 | 20.18 | 18.11 |

The opening inventory on March 1 was

| Liquor | $2,421.08 |
|---|---|
| Beer | 615.12 |
| Wine | 394.87 |

The actual closing inventory on March 7 was

| Liquor | $2,514.35 |
|---|---|
| Beer | 595.30 |
| Wine | 265.87 |

Prepare a blank daily liquor receiving and issues report and complete it from the information above for the week ending March 7. Comment on any differences discovered.

4. A club lounge had an opening total beverage inventory on April 1 of $4,116.20. Its closing total beverage inventory on April 30 was $3,917.80. During April beverage sales totaled $16,430, and it operated at a 30.5 percent beverage cost.

a. Calculate its beverage inventory turnover rate for April.

b. Would this be considered an acceptable result?

# 10

# Beverage Cost Control: The Bar

## Objectives

After studying this chapter, the reader will be able to

1. List and briefly explain each of the five steps in the cycle of beverage cost control using the potential cost control method, and given the appropriate information, calculate a potential cost percentage and an actual cost percentage.

2. Briefly explain the standard sales control method and, given appropriate information, calculate the standard sales value of a bottle of liquor using the weighted average technique and complete a standard sales control reconciliation.

3. Briefly describe the quantity (ounce) method of beverage cost control and, given appropriate information, complete the forms used with this method and make the calculations necessary for a reconciliation.

4. Complete a banquet liquor control reconciliation form.

5. Compare the results obtained using any of the above control methods with predetermined objectives and discuss whether or not the results are favorable.

The preceding chapter explained how control over the beverage storeroom can be accomplished by the use and periodic reconciliation of the daily liquor receiving and issues report. This chapter will deal with the control of the bar itself.

As is the case with food, it is impossible to have absolute control of every item issued from stores to the production area, in this case the bar. Even careless overpouring by a bartender who gives each customer 1/8 oz more than the standard measure of 1 oz may not seem like very much (nor is it even noticeable in the customers' glasses), but that 1/8 oz means 12 1/2 percent of all liquor used is being given away.

Similarly, if a dishonest bartender underpoured every 1 oz drink by 1/8 oz and sold every eighth drink without recording it on a sales check, he could substantially increase his income! In fact, in a bar averaging $30,000 a month (or $360,000 a year), the loss in revenue to the bar (and the increase in income to the bartender) would be $45,000 a year (12 1/2 percent of $360,000).

Despite the problems from this type of loss and from others, certain procedures can be instituted to show whether or not a bar is functioning well. These procedures will provide information that will indicate whether or not further investigation is required. Three of a number of different methods of control will be discussed here:

1. The potential cost control method
2. The standard sales control method
3. The quantity (ounce) control method

## 1. THE POTENTIAL COST CONTROL METHOD

The procedures for this method are similar to those outlined for food production control in Chapter 7:

1. Decide approximately what potential beverage cost percentage is desirable and attainable.
2. Establish standard recipes and drink sizes.
3. Calculate individual recipe costs.
4. Set selling prices that will give the cost percentage desired.
5. Periodically evaluate the actual results.

**Figure 10.1** A variety of methods are available for control of the bar. Photograph courtesy Hotel Vancouver, Vancouver, B.C.

## 1. Decide What Cost Percentage Is Desirable

Beverages of different types may have different markups. The markup on beer is usually lower than that on liquor, and the wine markup may be lower still. Because of this, costs and sales of these items, as explained earlier, should be kept separate. However, even in a single category—for example, liquor—some items are marked up higher (and thus have a lower cost percentage) than others. Cocktails, because of the extra labor and/or garnish involved, can generally sell at a higher price than the same quantity of liquor in a straight drink. If liquor is sold by the bottle, it will usually have a lower markup than would the contents of the bottle sold in individual drinks. For this reason, an establishment selling liquor by the bottle should keep the revenue and costs for such sales separate from all other liquor sales and costs (see Figure 10.2).

DAILY REPORT OF FULL BOTTLE SALES

Bar _Main_    Date _Nov. 8_

| Sales Check No. | Item | Quantity | Cost Unit | Cost Total | Sales Amount Unit | Sales Amount Total |
|---|---|---|---|---|---|---|
| 4370 | Harpers | 1 Quart | 5.25 | 5.25 | 12.00 | 12.00 |
| 5162 | Old Forrester | 1 Quart | 5.40 | 5.40 | 13.00 | 13.00 |
| 4759 | Can. Club | 2 Fifths | 4.75 | 9.50 | 11.00 | 22.00 |
| 3295 | Cutty Sark | 1 Fifth | 6.00 | 6.00 | 14.00 | 14.00 |
| | | | | | | |
| TOTALS | | | | 26.15 | | 61.00 |

Bar Manager _J. E. Bronz_

**Figure 10.2** A daily report of full bottle sales is used to keep a separate record of the total cost and total sales of these items.

| | | | COST | | SALES PRICE | | COST PERCENT | |
|---|---|---|---|---|---|---|---|---|
| BIN NO. | N A M E | DRINK SIZE | DRINK | BOTTLE | DRINK | BOTTLE | DRINK | BOTTLE |
| | | | | | | | | |
| | | | | | | | | |
| | | | | | | | | |
| | | | | | | | | |
| | | | | | | | | |
| | | | | | | | | |
| | | | | | | | | |
| | | | | | | | | |
| | | | | | | | | |
| | | | | | | | | |
| | | | | | | | | |
| | | | | | | | | |
| | | | | | | | | |
| | | | | | | | | |
| | | | | | | | | |
| | | | | | | | | |
| | | | | | | | | |
| | | | | | | | | |
| | | | | | | | | |
| | | | | | | | | |
| | | | | | | | | |
| | | | | | | | | |
| | | | | | | | | |
| | | | | | | | | |
| | | | | | | | | |
| | | | | | | | | |
| | | | | | | | | |
| | | | | | | | | |
| | | | | | | | | |

**LIQUOR PRICE LIST**
BY THE DRINK
AND
BY THE BOTTLE

**Figure 10.3** A form that could be used by the control office for summarizing cost and selling prices and cost percentages of all beverages served both by the drink and by the bottle.

## 2. Establish Standard Recipes and Drink Sizes

Drink recipes should show the quantities of liquor and other ingredients required for each separate drink or cocktail to ensure consistent quality and easy calculation of cost. The type and size of glass should be standardized—a 2 1/2 oz martini would look lost in a 5 oz glass, and the customer could think he was getting a short measure.

### 3. Cost Out Recipes

Once the quantities of ingredients have been determined, the recipes can be costed out. Note that food ingredients are also part of the cost of the drink. Obviously, as purchase prices of liquor and food change, recipe costs must be adjusted accordingly.

### 4. Set Selling Prices

When the selling price of each drink has been established, the cost percentage can be calculated. If the selling price used does not give a cost percentage that seems appropriate, changing the price or changing the quantities of ingredients used may bring the percentage in line with what is desired.

Copies of recipes should be kept at the bar for the information of all bartenders. A complete recipe for a gimlet, using three different types of liquor, appears below:

| Gimlet | Bar Gin | Beefeater Gin | Vodka |
|---|---|---|---|
| 1 oz lemon juice | $0.03 | $0.03 | $0.03 |
| 1 oz liquor | 0.20 | 0.30 | 0.25 |
| 1/4 oz Triple Sec | 0.06 | 0.06 | 0.06 |
| 1 slice lemon | 0.03 | 0.03 | 0.03 |
| 1 cherry | 0.02 | 0.02 | 0.02 |
| Total cost | $0.34 | $0.44 | $0.39 |
| Selling price | $1.30 | $1.50 | $1.30 |
| Cost of Sales | 26.2% | 29.3% | 30.0% |
| (Serve in 4 oz cocktail glass) | | | |

### 5. Evaluate Results Periodically

Once a week, or every two weeks or every month, evaluate the results by comparing the potential cost percentage with the actual cost percentage. A sales and potential cost analysis form is useful for this purpose (see Figure 10.4).

The figures in the Quantity Sold column are taken from the sales checks for the period. A tally, or scatter, sheet is used to

| SALES AND POTENTIAL COST ANALYSIS | | | Week ending _Dec./4_ | | |
|---|---|---|---|---|---|

| Item | Item | | Percent Cost | Quantity Sold | Total Cost | Total Sales |
|---|---|---|---|---|---|---|
| | Cost | Sale | | | | |
| Bar Scotch | 0.30 | 1.25 | 24.0 % | 870 | $ 261.00 | $1087.50 |
| Cutty Sark | 0.39 | 1.50 | 26.0 | 25 | 9.75 | 37.50 |
| Chivas Regal | 0.41 | 1.55 | 26.5 | 71 | 29.11 | 110.05 |
| Ballantine | 0.39 | 1.50 | 26.0 | 324 | 126.36 | 486.00 |
| Dewar | 0.40 | 1.50 | 26.7 | 104 | 41.60 | 156.00 |
| | | | | | | |
| Totals | | | | | $1,450.21 | $4651.75 |

Potential Cost Percent:   $\dfrac{\text{Total Cost}}{\text{Total Sales}} = \dfrac{1450.21}{4651.75}$ x 100 = _31.18 %_

Actual opening inventory              $2765.51

Add: purchases for week              1371.60
                                             $4137.11
Less: actual closing inventory       2666.82

Actual Cost                              $1470.29

Actual Cost Percent:   $\dfrac{\text{Actual Cost}}{\text{Total Sales}} = \dfrac{1470.29}{4651.75}$ x 100 = _31.61 %_

Difference      _0.43_

**Figure 10.4** This analysis form is used for developing a potential beverage cost percentage for comparison with the actual cost percentage.

add up the count of drinks sold (see, for example, Figure 8.8). The Total Cost and Total Sales amounts are obtained by multiplying the quantity sold by the drink Cost and Sale prices, respectively. The potential cost percentage calculated by dividing Total Cost by Total Sales and multiplying by 100, is the cost percentage we should have for this period for the quantities of drinks sold.

This potential cost percentage can then be compared with the actual cost percentage calculated, as shown on the form, using actual inventory and purchase figures. (Note that actual inventory amounts will include both storeroom *and* bar inventories; the purchases for the week amount can be taken from the related daily liquor receiving and issues report for that week. This latter figure must have added to it, from information taken from requisitions, any Transfers In [food items from the kitchen] and have subtracted from it any Transfers Out [wine for cooking]). Each week, the potential cost percentage and the actual cost percentage can be recalculated following this procedure.

Normally, if the actual result is within 0.5 percentage points of the potential figure, it would be considered satisfactory. In our case (see Figure 10.4 for the week ending December 14), the difference is less than that, so no further checking is necessary. If the difference is greater than 0.5 percentage points, it *cannot* be the result of a change in the sales mix (i.e., a change in the quantities of different types of drinks sold), because we have already taken this into consideration in our calculations. The difference can only be caused by such things as these:

Errors in inventory taking or inventory calculations

Over- or under-pouring of recipe quantities

Sales not all recorded on sales checks

Similar comparisons can be made for each separate bar location and for each category of beverage: liquor, beer, and wine. If full-bottle sales are made, these costs and sales can also be evaluated in the same manner, separate from the others.

## 2. THE STANDARD SALES CONTROL METHOD

A different approach to control of bar sales can be made using the standard sales method. This method converts the quantities of liquor used (according to inventory records) into standard sales dollars, and then these standard sales dollars are compared with actual sales dollars. It is particularly useful if sales checks are not used. As in the case of any type of bar control, this method calls for standard recipes and drink sizes.

For each type of liquor sold, we must calculate the standard sale value of a full bottle. In the case of some brands, this is relatively easy. A 32 oz bottle of bourbon in a bar serving 1 oz drinks at $1 each would have a standard sale value of

$$[32 \div 1] \times \$1 = \$32$$

A 25 oz bottle of Canadian rye from which 1 1/4 oz drinks were sold at $1.25 would have a standard sale value of

$$[25 \div 1 \ 1/4] \ X \ \$1.25 = \$25$$

## Standard Sales Value Using the Weighted Average Method

In most bars, however, liquor is dispensed from the bottle for different types of drinks, using different quantities per drink and different selling prices. To calculate the standard sale value in this case, the weighted average method can be used.

A test period is selected, preferably as long as possible to take care of weekly, monthly, and even seasonal influences. A count is made of the quantity of each type of drink sold during this test period. This information can then be used to calculate the standard sale value. In Table 10.1, the standard sale value of a bottle of bar gin is calculated to be $25.79.

But we now face another problem. Let us assume that $1.35 is the full price for a martini (as below). Our martini recipe calls for 1/4 oz vermouth in addition to the 1 1/4 oz gin. None of the selling price of $1.35 has been apportioned to the vermouth bottle. This would be all right if vermouth were used only in martinis, in which case the vermouth bottles would have a standard sale value of zero.

If any vermouth at all is sold in some other drinks, we

**Table 10.1**  Weighted Average Method (Brand: Bar gin, 25 oz per bottle)

| Type of Drink | Number Sold | Size of Drink | Total Ounces Sold | Drink Selling Price | Total Sales |
|---|---|---|---|---|---|
| Straight gin | 820 | 1 oz | 820 | $1.00 | $820.00 |
| Dubonnet cocktail | 60 | 3/4 oz | 45 | 1.25 | 75.00 |
| Gimlet | 80 | 1 1/2 oz | 120 | 1.25 | 100.00 |
| Pink Lady | 20 | 1 1/4 oz | 25 | 1.25 | 25.00 |
| Martini | 360 | 1 1/4 oz | 450 | 1.35 | 486.00 |
| Total | | | 1,460 | | $1,506.00 |

Total bottles sold $\dfrac{1{,}460 \ oz}{25 \ oz} = 58.4$

Standard sale value $\dfrac{\$1{,}506.00}{58.4} = \$25.79$ per bottle must take a different approach. Let us assume that we feature vermouth on the rocks in our bar at $1.20 for a 3 oz portion. The value of 1 oz is therefore $0.40, and the value of the 1/4 oz used in martinis is $0.10. It would then be necessary to recalculate the weighted average standard sale value of a bottle of bar gin using $1.25 as the selling price per martini.

In this illustration (Table 10.1), the Dubonnet cocktail (which contains 3/4 oz Dubonnet in addition to 3/4 oz gin) would have to be handled in a similar way. For drinks that combine liquor and cordials (liqueurs), the same approach can be used.

Once these calculations determining standard sales value per bottle have been made, these values will remain until changes occur in selling prices, or spot-checks show that the sales mix of a brand has changed. At this time, recalculations are necessary to assign new standard sales values.

Comparison between standard sales and actual sales can be made on a periodic (daily, weekly, monthly) basis by converting liquor used according to inventory records into standard sales dollars, and then comparing these expected (standard) sales with actual sales (see Figure 10.5).

In Figure 10.5, the Previous Inventory figure would be the same as the Present Inventory figure of the previous period's form. The Added per Requisitions column is completed by adding up the quantities recorded on requisitions for the period under review. Previous Inventory + Added per Requisitions = Total. The Present Inventory figures will come from an actual count of bottles and parts of bottles still on hand. Total – Present Inventory = Used. The figure in the Used column, multiplied by the Standard Sales Value column figure, will give the dollar amount to be entered in the Total Standard Sales column.

The final total standard sales dollar amount can then be compared with total actual sales (taken from sales records). A difference between the two results is to be expected. The standard sales values per type of liquor are based on a historical sales mix. The current period's mix may, and probably will, be different. As a guideline, it is suggested that the difference between the two should be no greater than 1 percent. In Figure 10.5, it can be seen that total standard sales were $4,615.23; 1 percent of this

| STANDARD SALES RECONCILIATION | | | | | Period from _Nov 1_ to _Nov 7_ | | | |
|---|---|---|---|---|---|---|---|---|
| Item | Size | Previous Inventory | Added per Requi-sitions | Total | Present Inventory | Used | Standard Sales Value | Total Standard Sales |
| Balance fwd. | | | | | | | | $ 1,878.29 |
| Bourbon Early Times | Q | 3.2 | 13.0 | 16.2 | 2.1 | 14.1 | 32.10 | 452.61 |
| Kentucky | Q | 2.4 | 13.0 | 15.4 | 3.7 | 11.7 | 34.70 | 405.99 |
| National | Q | 1.6 | 11.0 | 12.6 | 1.8 | 10.8 | 36.40 | 393.12 |
| Old Charter | Q | 4.7 | 10.0 | 14.7 | 3.2 | 11.5 | 32.10 | 369.15 |
| Harper | Q | 2.1 | 12.0 | 14.1 | 1.4 | 12.7 | 32.10 | 407.67 |
| Old G-Dad | Q | 1.9 | 12.0 | 13.9 | 2.1 | 11.8 | 34.00 | 401.20 |
| Old Taylor | Q | 0.4 | 11.0 | 11.4 | 1.8 | 9.6 | 32.00 | 307.20 |

| | |
|---|---|
| TOTAL STANDARD SALES | $ 4,615.23 |
| TOTAL ACTUAL SALES | $ 4,651.75 |
| VARIANCE | $ 36.52 |

**Figure 10.5** Reconciliation form used for converting liquor used into Total Standard Sales for comparison with Total Actual Sales.

is $46.15, so our actual result should be somewhere between $4,569.08 ($4,615.23 − $46.15) and $4,661.38 ($4,615.23 + $46.15). Our actual sales were $4,651.75, which is within the acceptable limit.

### Estimating Part Bottles

Note in Figure 10.5 that inventory of part bottles is recorded in tenths. Although this estimate is made by eye and is not necessarily accurate to the ounce, it is accurate enough for most practical control purposes.

### Full Bottle Sales

Since full bottle sales are made at a much lower markup than that for bottles sold as individual drinks, such sales should be kept separate from other liquor sales (see Figure 10.2). On our standard sales reconciliation form (Figure 10.5), the Used column would have to be reduced, where necessary, for such full bottle sales. Also, the Total Actual Sales figure would not include the sales from full bottles.

*Spillage*

Spillage allowance is a matter of individual establishment policy. Some establishments make no allowance for this. If an allowance of one or two ounces per bottle is permitted, then the calculation of the standard sales value for each brand of liquor would have to be adjusted accordingly by reducing the normal bottle size in ounces by the amount of spillage allowed.

## 3. THE QUANTITY (OUNCE) CONTROL METHOD

A useful technique for isolating the cause of an unacceptable difference between actual and potential (or standard) results is to use quantity, or ounce, control.

The method compares the quantity (in ounces) of each brand used according to inventory records with the quantity (in ounces) sold recorded on sales checks. Since the majority of sales in most beverage outlets is in liquor and most liquor sold is confined to the basic bar brands of bourbon, gin, rum, rye, scotch, and vodka, we can reduce the amount of checking involved by analyzing the results of only these items. (In many bars, these basic brands represent as much as 80 or 90 percent of all sales). Three records are required:

1. Inventory consumption record
2. Sales tally sheet
3. Summary of results

Figure 10.6 illustrates the inventory consumption record. Previous Inventory is copied from the Present Inventory column of the previous period's form. Previous Inventory + Added per Requisitions = Total. Total − Present Inventory = Total Used Bottles.

The Total Used Bottles figure is converted to Total Used Ounces by multiplying the Bottles figure by the bottle Size column figure. Note that part bottles of inventory are estimated in tenths—this speeds up the inventory-taking process, and will be found accurate enough for control purposes.

The sales tally sheet is illustrated in Figure 10.7. The quantities sold are taken from an analysis of sales checks for the

| INVENTORY CONSUMPTION RECORD | | | | Date _Nov. 7_ | | | |
|---|---|---|---|---|---|---|---|
| Item | Size | Previous Inventory | Added per Requisitions | Total | Present Inventory | Total Used | |
| | | | | | | Bottles | Ounces |
| Bourbon | 32 oz. | 10.4 | 6.0 | 16.4 | 8.1 | 8.3 | 266 |
| Gin | 32 oz. | 6.8 | 4.0 | 10.8 | 6.0 | 4.8 | 154 |
| Rum | 25 oz. | 7.1 | 5.0 | 12.1 | 4.9 | 7.2 | 180 |
| Rye | 25 oz. | 8.4 | 2.0 | 10.4 | 9.2 | 1.2 | 30 |
| Scotch | 26 oz. | 4.5 | 4.0 | 8.5 | 5.1 | 3.4 | 88 |
| Vodka | 32 oz | 9.2 | 2.0 | 11.2 | 6.4 | 4.8 | 154 |

**Figure 10.6** The inventory consumption record is used for converting amount of inventory used, by type of liquor, into Total Ounces Used.

period under review. Notice that not all drinks are the same size and that the Total Ounces Sold column is a multiplication of the Total column and the Drink Size column.

The results (Total Ounces Sold) are then transferred to the summary of results form (Figure 10.8). Note that liquor sold in cocktails or mixed drinks must be transferred to the relevant basic drink column (bourbon, gin, rum, rye, scotch or vodka). Once the columns on this sheet are added up, they can be compared with the related Total Ounces Used figures transferred from the inventory consumption record (Figure 10.6).

| SALES TALLY SHEET | | Date _Nov. 7_ | | | |
|---|---|---|---|---|---|
| Item | Quantity Sold | | Total | Drink Size | Total Ounces Sold |
| Bourbon | THL THL THL THL THL THL X | ‖ | 212 | 1 oz. | 212 |
| Gin | THL THL THL THL THL THL N | | 115 | 1 oz. | 115 |
| Rum | THL THL THL THL THL THL N | | 123 | 1 oz. | 123 |
| Rye | THL THL THL THL | | 20 | 1 oz. | 20 |
| Scotch | THL THL THL THL THL THL | | 89 | 1 oz. | 89 |
| Vodka | THL THL THL THL THL THL | | 124 | 1 oz. | 124 |
| Martini | THL THL THL THL THL THL | | 32 | 1¼ oz. | 40 |
| Manhattan | THL THL THL THL THL THL | | 40 | 1¼ oz. | 50 |
| Rye Sour | THL 1 | | 6 | 1½ oz. | 9 |
| Cuba Libre | THL THL THL THL THL THL | | 36 | 1½ oz. | 54 |
| Vodka Gimlet | THL THL THL THL THL 11 | | 27 | 1 oz. | 27 |

**Figure 10.7** The sales tally sheet summarizes drinks sold and converts drinks sold to Total Ounces Sold.

| SUMMARY OF RESULTS | | | Date | _Nov. 7_ | | |
|---|---|---|---|---|---|---|
| | SALES IN OUNCES | | | | | |
| | Bourbon | Gin | Rum | Rye | Scotch | Vodka |
| _Bourbon_ | 212 | | | | | |
| _Gin_ | | 115 | | | | |
| _Rum_ | | | 123 | | | |
| _Rye_ | | | | 20 | | |
| _Scotch_ | | | | | 89 | |
| _Vodka_ | | | | | | 124 |
| _Martini_ | | 40 | | | | |
| _Manhatten_ | 50 | | | | | |
| _Rye Sour_ | | | | 9 | | |
| _Cuba Libre_ | | | 54 | | | |
| _Vodka Gimlet_ | | | | | | 27 |
| _Total Ounces Sold_ | 262 | 155 | 177 | 29 | 89 | 151 |
| _Total Ounces Used_ | 266 | 154 | 180 | 30 | 88 | 154 |
| _Difference_ | -4 | +1 | -3 | -1 | +1 | -3 |

**Figure 10.8** The summary of results form compares Total Ounces Sold (see Figure 10.7) with Total Ounces Used (see Figure 10.6).

Differences between the two sets of figures will occur, primarily because of estimating part bottles in tenths of a bottle rather than in exact ounces. As long as these differences are only 2 or 3 ounces per type of liquor per day, it is acceptable. If differences are greater than this, further investigation may be necessary. For example, in Figure 10.8, the shortage of 4 ounces in sales of bourbon may be a bit high. The other brands are within the suggested limit.

## OTHER METHODS

### Banquet Liquor Control

The banquet department, if it has its own storage and bar area, can operate and be controlled in the same way as any other bar. If, however, for each separate function it must requisition beverages from the main beverage storeroom and then return any unused and partly used bottles to this storeroom, a special control form may be required.

Figure 10.9 is a sample of such a form. Bottles Issued would be the quantity issued from the beverage storeroom or main bar for that particular function. Bottles Returned are the bottles and part bottles unused at the end of the function. Bottles Issued − Bottles Returned = Bottles Used. Bottles Used x Cost (taken from the perpetual inventory card) = Total Cost. Drinks per bottle is the size of bottle (in ounces) divided by the size of drink served at the function. In the case illustrated, all drinks served were 1 ounce.

The Total Drinks column is completed by multiplying Bottles Used by Drinks per Bottle. The figures in this column could be checked against drink tickets sold for this function, if tickets are used. Total Drinks x Selling Price = Total Sales. This column total should agree with cash paid for drinks, if it is a cash bar. Alternatively, this column total would be the amount that the organization hosting the function will be billed.

| BANQUET LIQUOR CONTROL | | | | | | | Date | _Nov 7_ | | |
| Function | _Construction Association_ | | | | | | Room | _Ballroom_ | | |
| Item | Size | Bottles Issued | Bottles Returned | Bottles Used | Cost | Total Cost | Drinks per Bottle | Total Drinks | Selling Price | Total Sales |
|---|---|---|---|---|---|---|---|---|---|---|
| Bourbon | 32 oz | 12.0 | 2.1 | 9.9 | 5.00 | 49.50 | 32 | 317 | 1.00 | 317.00 |
| Gin | 32 oz | 3.0 | 0.4 | 2.6 | 4.75 | 12.35 | 32 | 83 | 1.00 | 83.00 |
| Rum | 25 oz | 4.0 | 1.3 | 2.7 | 5.25 | 14.18 | 25 | 68 | 1.00 | 68.00 |
| Rye | 25 oz | 6.0 | 0.8 | 5.2 | 5.75 | 29.90 | 25 | 130 | 1.25 | 162.50 |
| Scotch | 26 oz | 4.0 | 2.0 | 2.0 | 6.10 | 12.20 | 26 | 52 | 1.25 | 65.00 |
| Vodka | 32 oz | 8.0 | 1.9 | 6.1 | 4.50 | 27.45 | 32 | 195 | 1.00 | 195.00 |
| | | | | | | | | | | |
| Total Cost and Sales | | | | | | 145,58 | | | | 890.50 |
| Cost Percent | | | | | | $\frac{\text{Total Cost}}{\text{Total Sales}} = \frac{145.58}{890.50}$ x 100 = 16.35% | | | | |

Issued by _G V. Kay_     Returned by _a. Smith_

Issued to _a. Smith_     Returned to _G V. Kay_

**Figure 10.9** The banquet liquor control form is used when banquet liquor is obtained for each separate function from the main liquor storeroom. The form also permits calculation of a liquor cost percentage for each separate function.

**BANQUET REQUISITION AND RETURN REPORT**

NAME OF FUNCTION_____     DATE_____

ROOM_____ BAR_____ BANQUET CHECK NO. _____

| BIN NO. | NAME | UNIT | QUANTITY | | | COST | | ACTUAL SALES | | POT. SALES | |
|---|---|---|---|---|---|---|---|---|---|---|---|
| | | | ISSUED | RETURN | SOLD | UNIT | TOTAL | UNIT | TOTAL | UNIT | TOTAL |
| | | | | | | | | | | | |
| | | | | | | | | | | | |
| | | | | | | | | | | | |
| | | | | | | | | | | | |
| | | | | | | | | | | | |
| | | | | | | | | | | | |
| | | | | | | | | | | | |
| | | | | | | | | | | | |
| | | | | | | | | | | | |
| | | | | | | | | | | | |
| | | | | | | | | | | | |
| | | | | | | | | | | | |
| | | | | | | | | | | | |
| | | | | | | | | | | | |
| | | | | | | | | | | | |
| | | | | | | | | | | | |
| | | | | | | | | | | | |
| | | | | | | | | | | | |
| | | | | | | | | | | | |
| | | | | | | | | | | | |

REQUISITIONS:

Ordered by _____

Issued by _____

Received by _____

RETURNS:

Unused Stock Returned by_____

Received in Service Bar By_____

Wine Stewards Approval _____

**Figure 10.10** A form for use in the control of banquet liquor cost and sales.

| BANQUET BEVERAGE CONTROL | | | | | | | | |
|---|---|---|---|---|---|---|---|---|

Function_____  Date _____

Room_____  Bqt Ck. No. _____

Number in Party_____  Net Sales _____

Bartenders _____  Prov. Tax _____

Amt. billed _____

| | ISSUES | | | | CONSUMED | | | |
|---|---|---|---|---|---|---|---|---|
| Description | Units Issued | Additions | Total Issued | Returned | Units Used | Per Unit | Amount | |
| | | | | | | | | |
| | | | | | | | | |
| | | | | | | | | |
| | | | | | | | | |
| | | | | | | | | |
| | | | | | | | | |
| | | | | | | | | |
| | | | | | | | | |
| | | | | | | | | |
| | | | | | | | | |
| | | | | | | | | |
| | | | | | | | | |
| | | | | | | | | |
| | | | | | | | | |
| | | | | | | | | |
| | | | | | | | | |
| | | | | | | | | |
| | | | | | | | | |
| | | | | | | | | |
| | | | | | | | | |
| | | | | | | | | |
| | | | | | | | | |

| TICKETS | | RECAP | | |
|---|---|---|---|---|
| Last Number | | Units Consumed as Per Inventory | | |
| Starting Number | | Unit Used As Per Ticket Sales | | |
| Sold | | Difference | Over | |
| Used | | | Short | |
| Not Used | | Signature | | |
| Previously Sold | | | | |

**Figure 10.11** A form that could be used for control of banquet liquor when tickets are sold for drinks.

### Dispensers

*Metered*

    Mechanical dispensing devices, which measure each drink and count the number of drinks dispensed on meters for each pull of the dispensing trigger, are an aid to control because they reduce losses from human error (short pouring or overpouring).

They can also be used for a quick reconciliation of drinks sold against meter readings. For each separate installation, the cost of the investment must be weighed against the potential savings.

*Electronic*

The most recent advancement in liquor control is electronic dispensing of drinks. There are three principal features to the unit: a register, an electronic minicomputer, and a bottle rack/dispenser/compressor.

The register is similar to the preset precheck register described at the end of Chapter 2. Operation of the register, with a sales check inserted, automatically causes the minicomputer to print out the correct price on the sales check and activate the

**Figure 10.12** The register is one of the three elements of electronic bar equipment. By inserting a sales check and depressing the appropriate drink key, a computer connected to the register measures the liquor ingredients and dispenses them. The sales check is automatically printed with the appropriate drink description and price. Photograph courtesy The National Cash Register Company, Dayton, Ohio.

**Figure 10.13** The Electra Bar. Cartoon courtesy The National Cash Register Company, Dayton, Ohio.

dispenser to measure and dispense the correct liquor or liquors (in the case of mixed drinks).

As many as thirty-six different types of drinks can be dispensed in this fashion. Liqueurs and syrups, and any garnish, have to be added manually. An ounce counter in the minicomputer automatically adjusts the inventory downward as drinks are dispensed.

Such electronic dispensers can reduce human error and speed up the mixing and service of drinks (and, in some cases, do not require a professional bartender), but it is always necessary to weigh the cost of installation against the resulting benefits.

## SUMMARY

Control of the bar is more difficult than control of the beverage storeroom. A number of different methods were discussed in this chapter. The potential cost control method entails the following steps:

1. Decide approximately what potential beverage cost percentage is desirable and attainable.
2. Establish standard recipes and drink sizes.
3. Calculate individual recipe costs.
4. Set selling prices which will give the cost percentage desired.
5. Evaluate the results periodically.

The last item entails a comparison of the potential cost percentage at the end of each control period with the actual cost percentage. If the difference between the two is half of a percentage point or less, it is considered satisfactory. Greater difference might require investigation. Remember that a change in the sales mix cannot be the cause of any of the difference because we used the actual sales mix for the period to calculate both our potential and our actual cost percentages.

Another method of control, which still requires the implementation of the first four steps listed above, uses a different evaluation system. It is known as the standard sales control method. The quantities of liquor used (according to inventory records) are converted into standard sales dollars and then compared with actual sales dollars. Historical sales records are used to determine the standard sales values per type, or brand, of beverage. Because of this, the margin of tolerance between actual and standard sales dollars should be about 1 percentage point.

When taking inventory of the bar, part bottles are usually estimated in tenths. Full bottle sales should be separated out from both standard sales and actual sales.

Another method of control is quantity (or ounce) control. This method compares the quantity (in ounces) of each brand used according to inventory records with the quantity (in ounces) sold as recorded on sales checks. The method can usually be confined to the six basic bar types of liquor because in most bars these make up 80 to 90 percent of total sales volume.

A special control may be required for banquets if liquor is supplied from, and unused liquor returned to, one of the bars. To aid in bar control, both mechanical and electronic dispensing/control devices that measure and count each drink sold are available. The cost of installation of this type of equipment must always be weighed against the benefits (savings) that would occur.

## DISCUSSION QUESTIONS

1. What are the five steps in control of the bar using the potential cost control method?

2. Why should standard recipes and drink sizes be established?

3. Why do cocktails and other mixed drinks generally have a higher markup than straight drinks?

4. Briefly describe how the standard sales control method works.

5. Why is it sometimes necessary to use the weighted average method to determine the standard sale value of a type, or brand, of liquor?

6. What is the quantity (ounce) control method? Briefly describe how it operates.

*bourbon - of devils*
*list of*

## MULTIPLE CHOICE/DISCUSSION QUESTIONS

1. If a bartender carelessly overpours each one oz drink that he sells by 1/8 oz
   a. This proves that he is putting money into his own pocket.
   b. This means that sales will be 12 1/2 percent less than they should be.
   c. He should be told to be more careful and underpour drinks from that point on to compensate.
   d. It will mean that beverage cost will be 12 1/2 percent higher than it should be.
   e. It will mean that beverage cost will be 12 1/2 percent lower than it should be.

2. Liquor sales and costs for liquor sold by the bottle should be kept separate from sales and costs of liquor sold by the drink
   a. So that it is easier to use the quantity (ounce) method of control.
   b. Because in this way a liquor inventory turnover figure will be more meaningful.

c. To prevent a bartender from selling 25 individual 1 oz drinks and recording only a single sale of a full bottle.

d. To prevent a bartender from bringing in his own full bottles, selling them, and pocketing the revenue.

e. Because full bottles generally have a different markup and liquor cost results would otherwise be distorted.

3. The standard sales control method for liquor

a. Compares the potential cost percentage with the actual cost percentage.

b. Compares liquor used converted to standard sales dollars with actual sales dollars.

c. Compares quantity of liquor used according to inventory records with quantity sold according to sales checks.

d. Is only used in banquet situations.

e. Can only be used in cases where sales checks are also being used.

## PROBLEMS

1. The Liquid Lounge is being analyzed by the control office for the week ending December 10. Inventory at the beginning of the week was $1,250, purchases during the week were $1,163, and inventory at the end of the week is $1,213. Only a limited selection of drinks are sold in this bar. The cost, selling prices, and quantities sold during the week ending December 10 are as follows:

| Drink | Cost | Selling Price | Quantity Sold |
|-------|------|---------------|---------------|
| Gin | $0.20 | $1.00 | 1,008 |
| Rum | 0.25 | 1.10 | 300 |
| Scotch | 0.30 | 1.20 | 260 |
| Rye | 0.20 | 1.00 | 856 |
| Bourbon | 0.20 | 1.00 | 2,594 |
| Martini | 0.35 | 1.50 | 317 |
| Manhattan | 0.35 | 1.50 | 283 |

a. Calculate the potential cost percentage.

b. Calculate the actual cost percentage.

c. What is the difference between the two figures expressed as a percent change?

d. Would you be satisfied with this result?

2. The Elbow Bar uses the standard sales control method. From the following information, calculate the standard sales value of a 25 oz bottle of rye used in this bar, using the weighted average method.

| Drink | No. of Drinks Sold | Amount of Rye in Drink | Selling Price of Drink |
|-------|--------------------|------------------------|------------------------|
| Rye straight | 500 | 1    oz | $0.75 |
| Manhattan | 40 | 1    oz | 1.00 |
| Rye Alexander | 50 | 1 1/4 oz | 1.25 |
| Rye Sour | 20 | 1 1/2 oz | 1.25 |
| John Collins | 100 | 1 1/2 oz | 1.35 |

3. At the Knockemback Bar, which uses the standard sales control method, the following are the standard sales values in its specialty lounge, which serves only a limited selection of drinks.

Bourbon      $16.75

Gin            16.75

Rum           18.00

Scotch        18.50

Vermouth       9.00

An analysis of this bar is being made for January 6. Here are opening and closing inventory figures for that day, as well as bottles added (requisitioned) during that day:

| Type | Opening Inventory | Added | Closing Inventory |
|------|-------------------|-------|-------------------|
| Bourbon | 4.5 | 10.0 | 1.3 |
| Gin | 3.2 | 5.0 | 1.6 |
| Rum | 6.8 | 4.0 | 7.8 |
| Scotch | 4.1 | 3.0 | 5.2 |
| Vermouth | 2.0 | 1.0 | 2.6 |

Sales for the day were $410.20. Included in these figures is one full bottle of bourbon, which sold for $11.25.

a. Calculate total standard sales.

b. Would you be satisfied with this result?

4. A restaurant service bar uses the quantity (ounce) control method. The manager wishes to make a spot-check of rum sales records for comparison with rum inventory records on November 25. Opening rum inventory on that date was 6.4 bottles, and closing inventory was 4.1 bottles. Five full bottles of rum had been requisitioned from the storeroom on November 25. Bottles of rum contain 25 ounces. Analysis of sales checks revealed the following:

| Drink | Quantity Sold |
|-------|---------------|
| Straight rum ( 1 oz rum) | 144 |
| Daiquiri ( 1 1/2 oz rum) | 8 |
| Cuba Libre (1 1/4 oz rum) | 8 |
| Rum Swizzle (1 1/8 oz rum) | 8 |

As manager, would you be satisfied with these results?

5. A specialty bar serves only the following drinks. Alongside each drink is the quantity sold on December 11 according to a tally of the sales checks used that day.

| Drink | Quantity Sold |
|---|---|
| Bourbon | 244 |
| Gin | 36 |
| Rye | 24 |
| Scotch | 84 |
| Vodka | 44 |
| Martini | 64 |
| Manhattan (sweet) | 48 |

The five basic bar brands contain 1 1/4 oz liquor each. The Martini contains 1 3/4 oz gin and 1/4 oz dry vermouth. The Manhattan contains 1 3/4 oz bourbon and 1/4 oz sweet vermouth.

Inventory records for December 11 indicate the following:

| Item | Opening Inventory | Added | Closing Inventory |
|---|---|---|---|
| Bourbon | 5.1 | 16.0 | 4.5 |
| Gin | 4.2 | 4.0 | 2.0 |
| Rye | 9.7 | 0 | 8.5 |
| Scotch | 2.6 | 3.0 | 1.4 |
| Vodka | 3.8 | 1.0 | 2.6 |
| Dry vermouth | 2.4 | 0 | 1.9 |
| Sweet vermouth | 3.5 | 0 | 3.1 |

All bottles contain 25 oz except the two types of vermouth, which contain 32 oz. Using the quantity (ounce) control method, analyze these results and comment.

6. A banquet liquor control form indicated the following concerning a function held on May 6:

| Item | Bottles Issued | Bottles Returned | Cost of Bottle |
|---|---|---|---|
| Bourbon | 20.0 | 4.3 | $4.75 |
| Rye | 16.0 | 2.2 | 5.00 |
| Gin | 4.0 | 1.0 | 5.25 |
| Rum | 8.0 | 3.6 | 5.50 |
| Scotch | 6.0 | 0.9 | 6.50 |
| Vodka | 7.0 | 2.4 | 4.50 |

All bottles contain 25 oz; all drinks are 1 oz. Banquet liquor selling prices are $0.80 per drink except scotch, which is $1. Calculate the liquor cost percentage for this function.

7. You are the beverage comptroller for the Flamboyant Lounge. You have the following information about the operation of the bar for November 20:

| Item | Opening Inventory | Added per Requisitions | Closing Inventory |
|------|-------------------|------------------------|-------------------|
| Whisky | 3.1 bottles | 12.0 | 2.4 |
| Gin | 5.2 " | 8.0 | 3.7 |
| Rum | 6.0 " | 8.0 | 5.5 |
| Scotch | 3.8 " | 5.0 | 3.3 |
| Vermouth | 0.5 " | 1.0 | 1.1 |

Standard sales values have been calculated as follows:

| Item | Value |
|------|-------|
| Whisky | $27.00 |
| Gin | 27.50 |
| Rum | 25.00 |
| Scotch | 27.50 |

a. Note that these standard sales values are exclusive of any tax charged on individual drinks. Actual sales for the day are $987.60. Note that this amount includes a tax of 5 percent on each drink sold. Calculate total standard sales, compare with actual, and comment on the result.

b. You decide to investigate further by using the quantity (ounce) control method to determine what differences there are, if any, between usage and sale of each individual type of liquor. Analysis of sales checks reveals the following:

| Item | Drinks Sold |
|------|-------------|
| Whisky | 270 |
| Gin | 195 |
| Rum | 197 |
| Scotch | 126 |
| Martini | 24 |
| Manhattan | 16 |
| Double Martini | 4 |
| Daiquiri | 12 |
| Scotch Sour | 8 |

Whisky, gin, rum, and scotch drinks each contain 1 oz of the relevant liquor. A Martini contains 1 1/4 oz gin and 1/4 oz vermouth. A double Martini contains double the quantities of the single drink. A Manhattan contains 1 1/4 oz whisky and 1/4 oz vermouth. A Scotch Sour contains 1 1/2 oz Scotch. A Daiquiri contains 1 oz rum. All bottles contain 25 oz except vermouth, which has 32 oz. Comment on the results obtained.

8. Sales, including a 5 percent tax, in a cocktail lounge for one week were $1,915.40. Opening inventory was $143.77, and closing inventory, $184.95. Purchases during the week were $581.40. Only five types of liquor are purchased and sold in the bar:

| Liquor | Cost per Bottle |
|--------|-----------------|
| Whisky | $4.60 |
| Gin | 4.60 |
| Vodka | 4.55 |
| Rum | 4.70 |
| Scotch | 5.25 |

All bottles are of the 25 oz size. All drinks, whether straight or cocktails, contain only 1 oz of liquor. It is estimated that 90 percent of all drinks sold are straight drinks, with the following individual prices, including a tax of 5 percent:

| Drink | Price |
|-------|-------|
| Whisky | $0.70 |
| Gin | 0.70 |
| Vodka | 0.70 |
| Rum | 0.70 |
| Scotch | 0.75 |

Approximately equal quantities of each of these five brands are sold. Any soft drinks (mixers) served with the above are charged for at $0.05 a drink. Any cocktails served, although they contain only the basic 1 oz of liquor, are sold for $1, including the tax.

a. Calculate the bar's actual liquor cost percentage for the week.

b. Using the other information given above, comment about whether or not this is a satisfactory actual result, supporting your comment with calculations.

# Glossary

*Actual food (or beverage) cost:* What has actually been spent on food (or beverages) during a certain period of time (as opposed to potential food or beverage cost, which is what should have been spent). Actual cost is calculated as follows:

Actual opening inventory + purchases − actual closing inventory

*Actual food (or beverage) cost percentage:* Actual cost, divided by sales, and multiplied by 100.

*Actual inventory:* A physical count of food (or beverage) items actually on hand. Multiplying the count of each item by the item unit cost and totaling the results will give a total dollar value of actual inventory.

*À la carte:* A French term meaning that the menu price is for that item alone. No appetizer or dessert is included in the price. In some cases, even vegetables may be charged for additionally if they accompany the item.

*Average check (or cover):* The average amount spent by each guest in a particular meal period, day, week, month, or year. Is calculated by dividing total sales for that period by the number of guests served.

*Average inventory:* The average amount, in dollar value, carried in inventory during a period of time. It is calculated as follows:

[Opening inventory + closing inventory] ÷ 2

*Beverage cost:* See Food cost.

*Beverage cost percentage:* See Food cost percentage.

*Bin cards:* A simplified version of the perpetual inventory card. Used for keeping a running balance of what the actual count of items is in the storeroom; one card for each item.

*Blind receiving:* Delivery of goods with a packing slip showing no weights or quantities. This practice obliges the receiver to actually count or weigh all items received, and to record the quantities or weights on the packing slip.

*Canned food tests:* Tests carried out primarily to ensure that the best net weight yield is achieved after the liquid in which the food is packed has been drained.

*Charge sales checks:* Customers who do not pay cash for food or beverages are referred to as charge customers; their sales checks, signed by them and with an appropriate room number or credit card number recorded, are then part of accounts receivable.

*Convenience food:* Any food that has been partly or wholly prepared or precooked prior to purchase. A can of soup is a convenience food.

*Cooking loss:* A reduction in the weight of food as a result of cooking. Loss comes from evaporation and/or dripping. Generally, the higher the temperature at which the food is cooked, the greater the loss.

*Cooking, trim, and butchering tests:* Tests usually carried out on meat, poultry, and fish items to see which supplier can provide items that give the highest yield (after butchering, trim, and cooking) of the quality desired at the best price.

*Cost factors:* Numbers that can be calculated when meat is purchased in bulk and then butchered and trimmed on the premises. These factors (numbers) then permit quick recalculation of the butchered and trimmed cost per pound of meat when the supplier changes his bulk price. The general equation is

$$\frac{\text{Our calculated cost}}{\text{Supplier's price}} = \text{Cost factor}$$

These cost factors can be calculated per pound before cooking, per pound after cooking, or per portion. Multiplying the supplier's new price by the relevant cost factor quickly gives us the new cost per pound or per portion.

*Cost of sales:* See Food cost.

*Credit memorandum:* Form filled out when goods delivered have to be returned to the supplier for one reason or another. This form is signed by the delivery driver and is the establishment's proof that the goods were sent back. The supplier subsequently issues a credit invoice.

*Delivery hours:* Hours during which suppliers of food and beverages may deliver ordered goods to the establishment. These delivery hours should be restricted to the times when the establishment has a person on duty who can be officially designated as responsible for receiving goods.

*Delivery slip:* See Packing slip.

*Direct purchases:* Food purchases which are not put into a lockable storeroom upon receipt. These direct purchases are usually perishable, are generally stored in coolers or freezers close to the kitchen(s), and are considered as being put into production within the next twenty-four hours.

*Dry goods:* Generally food items that are not considered, in the short run, to be perishable. This includes such items as cereals and bottled and canned or other packaged goods. They are usually controlled in a lockable storeroom and issued, when required by production staff, by requisition only.

*Employee meals:* Employees working in food establishments are frequently entitled to free meals while on duty. The estimated cost of such meals should be separated out from the regular food cost. Even if employees have to pay for their meals, because they usually pay less than a regular customer eating the same food, the cost of these meals should be separated out. Any income from employee meals should also be shown separately from sales to regular guests. If costs (and sales, if any) of employee meals are not kept separate, a distorted food cost percentage may result.

*First-in/First-out:* A method of ensuring that items purchased at an earlier date than others are issued first. This reduces the possibility of spoilage.

*Food and beverage control office:* A branch of the accounting department.

*Food and beverage manager:* The person primarily responsible for the profitability of the food and beverage departments. The food and beverage control office personnel and the food and beverage manager must work closely and harmoniously together.

*Food (or beverage) cost:* Sometimes referred to as cost of goods sold. See Actual food (or beverage) cost.

*Food (or beverage) cost percentage:* See Actual food (or beverage) cost percentage.

*Food tests:* See Canned food test; Cooking, trim and butchering tests; Fruit and vegetable tests.

*Fruit and vegetable tests:* Tests carried out to ensure that the best count or weight consistent with quality desired is received for money spent.

*Gross profit:* Food (or beverage) sales less food (or beverage) cost.

*Information system:* A system of procedures, forms, and reports to provide information to management so that decisions can be made and appropriate action taken where and when required.

*Inventory:* See Actual inventory.

*Inventory turnover:* The rate of turnover of inventory of food (or beverages). The general equation for expressing this turnover is

$$\frac{\text{Food (or beverage) cost for the month}}{\text{Average food (or beverage) inventory}}$$

Turnovers are usually calculated on a monthly basis and range from two to four times a month for food, and half to one time a month for beverages.

*Journal sheets:* Forms that present accounting information in a columnar arrangement. In food and beverage control they will be found particularly useful for recording information manually from sales checks so that sales can be summarized and totals quickly calculated.

*Markup:* The amount by which the cost of an item is increased to arrive at a selling price. The difference in dollars between selling price and cost is known as gross profit.

*Meat tag:* A two-part, perforated tag that aids in the control and use of meat.

*Memorandum invoice:* Food (or beverage) deliveries are generally accompanied by an invoice. If an invoice is inadvertently forgotten by the supplier, the receiver can make out a "memorandum invoice" when he receives the goods. This is a blank piece of paper on which he records relevant information (supplier's name, quantity or weight of each item, and brief description of the item). It can be used until the actual invoice is received.

*Most recent price:* A simple, although not necessarily completely accurate, method of recording unit costs of food items on perpetual inventory cards. As each new delivery is received, the item price from the invoice is recorded on the card. From that point on, all previous prices (costs) on the card are ignored. All items still in the storeroom of that type and size are subsequently costed out at the new, most recent, price on requisitions.

*Net sales:* The amount of sales revenue (food or beverages) excluding tax.

*Open stock inventory:* The amount of all food inventory not in the storeroom.

*Packing slip (delivery slip):* A document the supplier sends with goods. The packing slip carries a brief description of the goods and the quantity or weight. It is separate from the invoice, which is a more formal document and includes cost information.

*Par stock:* The maximum quantity of a food or beverage item that should be on hand to take care of normal production requirements. When goods are ordered from suppliers or requisitioned from the storeroom, the amount ordered or requisitioned should be the amount required to bring stock back up to this predetermined par level.

*Perishables:* Items of a perishable nature generally purchased on a daily basis, such as fruit, vegetables, bakery and dairy goods, and sometimes even meat, fish, and poultry.

*Perpetual inventory card:* A useful control form for storeroom items completed daily from invoices and requisitions. There should be one card for each separate type or size of item in stores. The card gives, among other things, a running (perpetual) balance of the count of items there should be in the storeroom.

*Physical inventory:* See Actual inventory.

*Portion control:* The establishment of the quantity or weight that should be served for each separate menu item to ensure consistency. Portion control also refers to a system of control of food items purchased in prepackaged individual containers (i.e., purchasing ketchup in tinfoil packets instead of in large bottles) and to purchase of meat items in prebutchered portions of specified weight or size which can be more easily controlled than the bulk purchase of meat with subsequent on-premise butchering.

*Portion size:* See Portion control. The portion size should be incorporated in the standard recipe.

*Potential food (or beverage) cost:* The estimated, anticipated, or expected cost to generate a given amount of sales. This will seldom be the same as the actual cost calculated from inventory and purchase records.

*Potential food (or beverage) cost percentage:* Potential cost, divided by sales, and multiplied by 100 equals potential cost percentage.

*Quotation:* Price of an item given (quoted) by a possible supplier.

*Receipt stub:* A perforated section of a sales check numbered to correspond with the sales check. As a waiter or waitress turns in cash from the customer to the cashier in payment of a sales check, the cashier can validate this receipt stub and give it back to the server. This stub then becomes the server's proof that the cash has been turned in to the cashier.

*Receiving stamp:* A rubber stamp used to validate each invoice received. The stamp provides a space for the receiver, or other person responsible, to indicate with a signature that goods received and described by the invoice are acceptable insofar as quantity and quality is concerned, and that the price on the invoice agrees with the supplier's quotation.

*Recipes:* See Standard recipes.

*Requisition:* A form that permits a department (kitchen, dining room, bar) to order (requisition) needed supplies from the storeroom. Requisitions can also be used for interdepartmental transfers—for example, to permit the bar to obtain eggs and fruit from the kitchen.

*Revenue:* See Sales.

*Sales:* The money collected (or to be collected in the case of charge sales) from customers in the food and beverage dining room(s) and bar(s).

*Sales check:* The document on which a waiter or waitress records what a guest orders. The server can subsequently price the items and extend and add up the check for presentation to the guest for payment.

*Sales check duplicates:* Duplicates of sales checks used primarily for ordering food from the kitchen and/or beverages from the bar.

*Sales mix:* The quantity of each separate menu item that customers buy. A change in preferences will change the sales mix, which in turn can cause a change in the food cost percentage.

*Scatter sheet:* See Tally sheet.

*Server:* A waiter or waitress.

*Spillage allowance:* A discretionary amount of liquor that management may permit bartenders to not account for in sales. In other words, if 1 oz drinks are the standard size, then only 24 drinks out of a 25 oz bottle must be accounted for. The 1 oz "allowance" will take care of an occasional spilled drink or accidential overpouring.

*Specifications:* Guidelines given to suppliers, primarily concerning the quality of goods on which they are invited to quote a price.

*Spot-checks:* Occasional checks of certain control forms or procedures to ensure that the control system is being followed correctly.

*Staff meals:* See Employee meals.

*Standard recipe:* A written formula detailing ingredient quantities needed to produce a certain quantity and quality of a menu item. The formula includes cooking method and portion size.

*Standing orders:* Orders given to suppliers directing them to deliver specific quantities of certain perishable items each day. Standing orders eliminate the necessity of telephoning suppliers each day.

*Storeroom purchases:* Puchases put into a storeroom under lock and key to be issued by requisition only.

*Table d'hôte:* A fixed-price meal, the price of which generally includes an appetizer, dessert, and beverage.

*Tally sheet (scatter sheet):* A form listing menu or drink items and on which can be recorded, from information taken from sales checks, the quantity sold of each item during a specific period.

*Yield:* What is available of a food product for sale to customers after the product has been trimmed, boned, and cooked.

# Index